Housing Rights Guide

(1989-90 EDITION)

by Geoffrey Randall

SHAC

189a Old Brompton Road, London SW5 0AR

SHAC

SHAC opened in 1969 as London's first independent housing aid centre. Its work covers the whole range of housing problems, including homelessness, security of tenure, disrepair and mortgage arrears. Over the past 20 years SHAC has given advice and help to over 120,000 households.

SHAC's publications and training courses draw on this direct advice-giving experience; it produces a range of advice booklets, publishes research into major housing issues and provides information and training for a wide range of voluntary and statutory organisations.

For further information about SHAC **publications**, contact the Publications Officer; for details of **training courses**, contact the Training Department (both at the address below).

GEOFFREY RANDALL is an independent housing and research consultant.

Acknowledgements

This guide has been produced with the advice and help of many people. In particular I would like to thank KEN BAUBLYS, MARTIN CANTOR, JOHN GALLAGHER, CHRISTINE JAMIESON, EDMUND JANKOWSKI, PETER KEMP, JAN LUBA, SUE LUKES, JOHN McQUILLEN, NICK RAYNSFORD, RIZWAN RAZAQ, BARRY SIMONS, SUE WITHERSPOON and JOHN ZEBEDEE. Their help has been invaluable, but responsibility for any omissions or errors is the author's.

ISBN 0 948857 25 0

1st Edition March 1985
Reprinted August 1985
2nd Edition November 1986
3rd Edition March 1989

Contents

Introduction 11

1 Finding A Home

Renting from the council 14

The housing list 15

If you are homeless 16

who is homeless; who the council will house; who is in priority need; who is intentionally homeless; if you are not in priority need; where to go if you are homeless; which council to go to; the council's investigations; what kind of housing the council will provide; challenging the council's decision

Other rights to rehousing 21

Other council housing schemes 21

hard-to-let; key worker schemes; schemes for special groups; the elderly

The council's offer of a home 22

Moving to another council house 24

transfers; exchanges; mobility schemes; key worker schemes; housing for industry scheme

Moving to a new town 27

Renting from a private landlord 27

Where to look 28

Negotiating the tenancy agreement 28

Renting from a housing association 29

Moving to another area 30

Renting from a housing co-operative 30

Setting up your own co-op 31

Buying a home 32

Getting a mortgage loan 32

How much you can borrow 34

Which type of mortgage to choose 34

The cost of buying a home 36

The steps to buying a home 38
finding a property; negotiating the purchase; applying for a mortgage; the legal steps

Low cost home ownership schemes 41
shared ownership schemes; leasehold for the elderly; rental purchase; homesteading; other low cost schemes

Temporary and emergency housing 43

Hostels 43

Women's refuges 44

Bed and breakfast hotels 44

Squatting 44

Short life housing 45

Race and sex discrimination 46

Racial discrimination 46
what is discrimination; discrimination by accommodation agencies and landlords; small premises; discrimination against existing tenants; inducing or helping others to discriminate; estate agents; action against racial discrimination

Sex discrimination 48
direct discrimination; indirect discrimination: victimisation; action against sex discrimination

2 Keeping Your Home

Private tenants and licensees 50

Tenant or licensee? 51

Tenancies which began before 15 Janaury 1989 52

Tenancies which began before 15 January 1989 but which are not fully protected by the Rent Act 1977 53

Regulated tenants; protection from eviction 56
contractual and statutory tenancies; Notice to Quit; grounds for eviction; discretionary and mandatory grounds for possession

Tenants with restricted contracts 60
protection from eviction; lettings made before 28.11.80; lettings made on or after 28.11.80
Protected Shorthold tenancies 62
Tied housing: a home with a job 63
service occupiers; service tenants
Tied housing: agricultural workers 64
protected occupiers; farm workers not protected by the Rent (Agriculture) Act 1976
Assured tenancies which began before 15 January 1989 67
Tenancies which began on or after 15 January 1989 67
Assured tenancies excluded from protection 67
Assured tenants: protection from eviction 68
Assured shorthold tenancies 71
Tenants with resident landlords 72
Assured agricultural occupancies 72
All Tenants 72
Tenants with only basic protection 72
Sharers 73
Tenants of landlords with mortgages 75
Licensees: protection from eviction 75
licensees with restricted protection: licensees without restricted protection
Going to court 76
The eviction 78
illegal evictions and harassment
The key questions for private tenants 78

Council tenants, housing association tenants and tenants of other public landlords 79
Housing Association tenants 79
Secure tenants 79
protection from eviction

Home owners 86
Mortgage arrears 86
Action by the local council 86
Long leaseholders: protection from eviction 86

Mobile homes 87
Protection from eviction 87
The right to a written agreement and statement of rights 88
Other rights to mobile home owners 88
Settling disputes 89

Squatters 89
Getting a possession order from the court 89
Eviction by someone living in or entitled to live in the property 90
Forcible eviction of squatters 90

3 Paying For Your Home and Reducing Your Housing Costs

Private Tenants 91
Fair rents for regulated tenants 91
applying to the Rent Officer
Reasonable rents for tenants and licensees with restricted protection 94
Rents for assured shorthold tenants 95
Service charges in flats for private and housing association tenants and owner occupiers with long leases 96
the right to be consulted; the right to information on service charges; the right to challenge unreasonable charges; action through a tenants' association

Council tenants 99
Rents 99
Rent arrears 99
distraint or distress for rent arrears

Housing association tenants 100
Rents 100
Rent arrears 100

Home owners 100
Choosing the right mortgage 100
Tax relief on mortgage interest payments 100

The homeloan scheme 101

If you are not working or work less than 24 hours a week 101

Cutting mortgage costs 102

capital repayment mortgages; endowment mortgages; if you have two or more mortgages

Mortgage arrears 103

Service charges in flats 103

Housing benefit 103

People on income support 104

tenants; heating and other fuel charges

People not on income support: rent allowances, rent rebates and rate rebates 105

how rent allowances, rent rebates and rate rebates are calculated

All claimants; how housing benefit is paid 107

How long housing benefit lasts 107

If you are away from home 108

Appealing against the assessment of housing benefit 108

Special arrangements for students 109

Housing benefit: the figures 110

People in hostels, bed and breakfast hotels and lodging houses 114

People with no homes at all 115

A special note for people from abroad 115

4 Improving Conditions in Your Home: Repairs, Improvements and Overcrowding

Private and housing association tenants 117

Legal rights to repair 117

local councils' powers and duties under Public Health Acts and Housing Acts; unfit properties; right to rehousing and compensation if your home is closed or demolished; if your home is not unfit but is in need of repair

Enforcing your rights to repair 122
getting the council to require your landlord to do repairs; taking action yourself against the landlord: Housing Act 1961, Public Health Act 1936, Defective Premises Act 1972

Using the rent to pay for the repairs 126

Getting improvements done 127
housing action areas and general improvement areas; doing improvements yourself

Overcrowding 129
the room standard; the space standard

Houses in multiple occupation 131
facilities; overcrowding; means of escape from fire; management and control; councils' use of their powers

Housing association tenants: action through a tenants' association 133

Housing association tenants: a new 'right to repair' 133

Council tenants 133

Putting extra pressure on the council 135

Taking action yourself 135

Doing minor repairs yourself 136

People in council temporary accommodation 137

Improvement, repairs and insulation grants for home owners, tenants and landlords 138

Types of grants 138

Who can claim a grant 138

How much is the grant? 140

After the improvement work 142

Insulation grants 142

5 Other Rights of Tenants

Private tenants 143

Harassment and illegal eviction 143
who is protected; what to do

When a tenant's family can inherit the tenancy 145

The right to a rent book and receipts for rent 145

When the landlord can enter your home 146

Not wanting the landlord's improvements 146
A list of furniture 147
No children allowed 147
Changing the tenancy agreement 147
Fuel costs: what landlords can charge 148

Private tenants and long leaseholders 148
Buying the freehold of the building from the landlord 148
Changing the lease 149
The right to know the name of the landlord 149

Council and housing association tenants 149
The right to inherit the tenancy 149
The right to take in lodgers and tenants 150
Passing on the tenancy to someone else 151
The right to exchange with another tenant 151
The right to make improvements to your home 151
The right to be consulted by the landlord 152
Changes to the tenancy agreement 152
Rights to information 152
The right to buy 152

6 Housing Rights and Relationship Break Up

In an emergency 155
Going to a women's refuge 155
Going to the council 155
Getting an injunction 156

Long-term rights to the home 158
If you are married 158
If you are not married 160
tenants; home owners
Money problems 162
maintenance; rent arrears; mortgage arrears; loss of income

Custody of children 162
Key points to remember 163

7 Getting Advice and Legal Representation

General advice 164
Housing advice centres 164
Other specialist advice 165
Solicitors 166
The Legal Aid Scheme 166
The Green Form Scheme 166
Legal aid under a Legal Aid Certificate 167
The Law Society's Charge 167
Campaigning to change policies 168

Appendix I: Useful publications 170
Appendix II: Useful addresses 174
Notes 186
Index

Introduction

Since the first edition of the *Housing Rights Guide* was published in 1985 it has become established as a key reference book for advisers and for people with housing problems.

This 1989 third edition of the *Housing Rights Guide* contains much new material, including details of the wide ranging changes brought about by the Landlord and Tenant Act 1987, the Housing Act 1988 and the extensive social security and housing benefit changes introduced in April 1988.

Most people will have a housing problem at some time in their lives. You may have a problem over finding a home to rent or buy, over repairs, or paying the rent or mortgage, or over rights to stay in the home if the landlord or your partner wants you to leave. Yet until the first edition of the *Housing Rights Guide* was published there was no comprehensive and up-to-date guide to help people sort out these problems. There were leaflets and guides about a wide range of separate problems, but the only comprehensive books available were aimed at lawyers and housing experts. This guide gives essential information on finding, paying for, keeping and repairing a home. In addition to an outline of the law it gives practical guidance on how to resolve problems. This third edition has been completely revised and updated. Housing law is extremely complicated and in a guide such as this it is necessary to leave out many of the details. People who want to check on their rights can use this guide as a starting point, but if the problem is complicated they are strongly advised to seek further help from one of the organisations listed in Chapter 7.

Chapter 1 gives information on finding a home including:

- How to apply for a council house, what rights the homeless and other groups of applicants have to a home and how applicants and tenants can move to other areas.

- How to look for a private rented home, what accommodation agencies are allowed to charge and what to look out for when agreeing a tenancy, including the extra charges landlords can make.

- How to apply for a home to rent through a housing association or tenants' co-operative.

- How to go about buying a home including how to raise the money, what pitfalls to look out for and details of new low cost home ownership schemes.

- How to find emergency short-term housing if you are homeless including information on hostels, bed and breakfast hotels, short life housing and squatting.

- What to do if you meet with racial or sex discrimination.

Chapter 2 gives details of the rights of people who are threatened with eviction from their homes including all types of tenants, owners, people living in mobile homes and squatters. It includes full details of the new types of tenancy introduced by the Housing Act 1988.

Chapter 3 gives information on how to reduce your housing costs and how to get help with paying for your home. It includes separate sections for private, council and housing association tenants, for owners and for people living in hostels. It also includes details of the new housing benefit scheme introduced in April 1988.

Chapter 4 gives information on tenants' rights to get repairs and improvements to their homes and on renovation grants for owners.

Chapter 5 contains details of the wide range of other rights available to tenants and long leaseholders whether their landlord is a private owner, the council or a housing association, including what information landlords must give tenants, what to do if the landlord is harassing you, how much landlords can charge for services and many other rights of tenants. It includes full details of the major changes introduced by the Landlord and Tenant Act 1987 and the Housing Act 1988.

Chapter 6 is for people whose marriage or relationship has broken down and gives information on rights to stay in the home and the rights of battered women.

Chapter 7 tells you where to go for further advice and help.

Although the information in this guide might sometimes appear complex, it must be emphasised that it does offer only an introduction to and broad outline of the law. Anyone unsure of their rights should seek further advice, which is often available free of charge. Throughout the guide the points on which it is particularly important to get advice are identified. Chapter 7 gives details of where to go for this advice.

The laws described in this guide apply to England and Wales only. Housing law changes fairly frequently; the information here is on the law at January 1989. Numbered references to specific legislation and regulations in the text can be found in the notes on page 186. Legal and technical terms are usually explained the first time they appear in the text. The pages on which these explanations appear are indicated in bold type in the index.

1: Finding a home

Renting from the council

About one in three homes in this country are rented from local councils although this number is likely to decline over the next few years. It is often thought that to get a council house applicants have to join a queue, as if waiting for a bus, and then await their turn. But this is a misleading picture. In reality, some people's need for a home is greater, or more urgent, than others' and councils have to take account of this in deciding who should be offered a home first. For example, someone who has only just joined the housing list but has no home at all might be given higher priority than other applicants who have been on the list for several years but who already have a home of some kind.

Local councils have a legal duty to find housing only for certain limited groups of people; for the rest councils can effectively decide who should get priority in their own areas. In most areas there is a shortage of council housing and there are many more people applying than can be offered a home. This section describes how councils decide on their priorities and who has a legal right to housing. Councils are obliged by law to publish details of how they make these decisions. This is known as their *allocation scheme* and you have a right to see a copy of these published details.[1*]

You should find out from the town hall or local council offices how to make an application for housing. Their telephone number will be in the directory or you can get it from a local library. Normally you will get a form from the housing department of the council and will have to give details of yourself, your family if any and your present housing conditions. In London there is a legal right to register on the housing list of the area in which you live.[2] You should not be put off even if the council tells you it is pointless to register. Outside London some councils do not allow certain groups of people to register. They might for example prohibit single people under a certain age or home owners from registering, or you might have to have lived in an area for a number of years before being allowed to register. However, registering on

*Numbered notes in the text refer to details of specific regulations and legislation for advisers who need to examine the law in more detail. See page 186.

the list is only one way of getting council housing. If you are homeless the council may have to house you directly (see page 16).

If you are being actively considered for an offer of housing you will probably be visited by someone from the council to check on your details. Some councils still use this visit to check also on people's 'housekeeping standards'. People judged to have 'high standards' may well be offered one of the better quality homes.

It is often necessary to re-register each year and when you put your name on the list you should check when you have to renew your application.

THE HOUSING LIST

Councils keep a list of people who apply for housing. This is sometimes called a 'waiting list' although this is a very misleading term, since length of time on the list is usually only one of the factors that might be taken into account in deciding who gets housed. There are four ways in which councils decide who goes to the top of the list. They often use a combination of these schemes.

- *Points schemes:* These are very commonly used by councils. The aim of points schemes is to assess the level of need of applicants by giving a number of points for different housing problems and then adding them together. Points are given for such factors as overcrowding, lack or shared use of bathroom or WC, bad conditions, poor health which is affected by the housing conditions, and length of time spent on the list or in the area. So, for example, a family might be given 30 points because they are short of a bedroom, 20 points because their home is in a bad state of repair, 10 points because they have no hot water, 20 medical points because dampness in the home affects their bronchitis and two points for spending one year on the list, making a total of 82 points. The people with the highest points will be at the top of the housing list.

- *Group schemes:* These schemes put applicants into different groups and then allocate a number of homes to each group. These groups might be based on the type of household, for example single people, families or the elderly; or might relate to types of housing need, for example overcrowing or bad conditions.

- *Date order schemes:* At their simplest these are like the bus queue: first come, first served.

- *'Merit' schemes:* These schemes, now rare, depend on a subjective assessment of each case 'on its merits'. The assessment might be made by council officers, elected councillors or both.

In practice many authorities use a combination of these schemes in deciding who will be offered housing. So, for example, applicants might be sorted first into groups, such as families with children or the elderly, and then given points within each group. Or the council might house people in 'date order' but have special provisions for people in certain groups, such as urgent medical cases, to go to the top of the list. When you register on the list your local authority should tell you how it will assess your application.

IF YOU ARE HOMELESS

Local councils have a legal duty under the Housing Act 1985 to help people who are homeless or who are threatened with homelessness. For some groups of homeless people the council has to find a permanent home, but for others the council may only have to find temporary accommodation or perhaps only provide them with advice and general help.

Who is homeless or threatened with homelessness

Under the Housing Act 1985 people count as homeless if:[3]

- they have no accommodation they are entitled to occupy, **or**
- they have a home but are in danger of violence from someone living there, **or**
- they are living in accommodation meant only for an emergency or crisis (for example a night shelter), **or**
- they are a family who are normally together but are now living in separate homes because they have nowhere to live together, **or**
- their accommodation is moveable (for example a caravan or houseboat) and they have nowhere to place it, **or**
- they have accommodation but it is not reasonable to continue to occupy it.

People are considered as being *threatened with homelessness* if they are likely to become homeless within 28 days.

Who the council will house

Not all people who are homeless or threatened with homelessness are provided with a home by the council. The council is, however, under a legal obligation to make sure that homeless people have somewhere to live if:

- they are in *'priority need'* **and**

- they did not make themselves *'intentionally homeless'.*

What is meant by 'priority need' and 'intentionally homeless' is explained in the next two sections.

Who is in priority need

The following groups of people are counted as being in priority need:[4,5]

- people who have dependent children aged either under 16, or under 19 if they are receiving full time education or training;
- all pregnant women;
- people who are homeless because of a fire, flood or similar emergency;
- people who are vulnerable because of
  - — old age
  - — mental illness or handicap
  - — physical disability
  - — other special reasons.

Local councils can decide who is 'vulnerable', but should always accept people over retirement age. Some will also accept people approaching retirement age if they are in poor health. Some councils will accept battered women without children and young people at risk. Although councils have discretion in deciding who is 'vulnerable', they must act reasonably and unreasonable decisions have been successfully challenged (see page 20, *Challenging the council's decision*).

Who is intentionally homeless

If the council decides you are *intentionally homeless* this means that it is satisfied that you have given up accommodation you could have continued to live in, or that you have lost accommodation through your own fault (for example, by not paying the rent).[6] Events that happened some time in the past may be taken into account if the council decides that these are the main cause of your homelessness. However, once again, councils must act reasonably and take all the facts into account. For example, if rent arrears were not deliberate and arose because of circumstances beyond your control you should not be treated as intentionally homeless. Councils' decisions can sometimes be successfully challenged and overturned. If you are intentionally homeless the council does not have to find you a permanent home, **but if you are in priority need it**

is still under a duty to find you somewhere to live temporarily and to give you advice and help with finding your own accommodation.[7]

If you have a home but are about to lose it, it is very important that you stay there for as long as you are entitled to. If you leave earlier, the council might decide you are intentionally homeless. In some circumstances this might mean waiting until you get a court order to evict you. If you are in danger of homelessness always get advice before leaving your home.

If you are not in priority need

If you are homeless but not in priority need, for example if you are a healthy person under retirement age without children, then the council does not have a legal duty to find you a home. It does, however, have to provide you with *advice and assistance.*[8] In practice this might be not much more than printed information on local hostels, cheap hotels and accommodation agencies; but some councils give more help than this and some might offer a home even if you are not legally in priority need, so it is always worth applying to the council.

Where to go if you are homeless

If you are homeless or likely to be homeless in the near future, you should go to the Homeless Persons Section of the council. This will often be in the housing department. If you do not know where to find it, ask at the town hall or local council offices. When you get there make sure that you are seen by someone from the Homeless Persons Section. Some councils call it by a different name; for example, Homeless Families, Housing Emergency or Housing Welfare Section. Sometimes you will be seen by someone from the Housing Aid or Advice Section first. Tell the person you see that you are homeless or about to become homeless. Make it clear that you need help urgently and have not come just to put your name on the housing list. Try to get the name of the person you see as you may need to speak to them again.

Do not be put off if the council is unhelpful. Remember you have a legal right to be given help and the council has a legal duty to provide it.

Which council to go to[9]

Usually you should go to the council in the area where you become homeless or are about to become homeless. However, long-term help for people in priority need will normally be given by a council with which they have a *'local connection'.* Generally, you should be considered as having a local connection with a council if you, or anybody who normally lives with you:

- have lived in the council's area for six months out of the past year, or three years out of the past five, **or**

- have a permanent job in the area, **or**
- have close family who have lived in the area for at least five years, **or**
- have any other special connections with the area, for example you were brought up there.

But residence with, or employment by, the armed forces does not count as local connection, nor does residence in a prison, hospital or other institution if you are detained in one of these.

If you apply to a council with which you (or anybody who lives with you) have any of these local connections then that council should be responsible for helping you.

If you have no local connection with the council to which you apply, that council must investigate your case and decide whether you are homeless, and in priority need, and whether you are intentionally homeless. If it decides you have a right to help, but that you have no local connection with that council, then it can contact another council with which you do have a local connection, to make sure that it will help you. If you have a local connection with more than one other council and you would prefer to live in a particular area then your wishes should be taken into account, so it is important to make them clear. The council that you first apply to must make sure that the other council will help you; it **must not** simply send you along there. If you have nowhere to stay while these arrangements are being made, then the council that you first applied to must make sure that you have temporary accommodation.

If you have no local connection with any area then the council to which you first apply has the duty to help you. People in fear of domestic violence, such as battered women, must never be sent back to the area from which they have fled unless the council is satisfied that there is no risk of violence if they return to that area. The council should take account of your own fears of violence. If you think that it has not, get advice.

The council's investigations

When you ask a council for help because you are homeless the council will check:

- whether you are homeless;
- whether you are in priority need;
- whether you are homeless intentionally;
- whether you have a 'local connection' with the area.

These investigations often involve detailed questions about your personal life. People who make false statements or withhold relevant information can be prosecuted and fined up to £1,000.[10]

If you have nowhere to stay while the council is checking your story, it must make sure you have somewhere to live until it reaches a decision.[11] If it decides that it does not have a duty to find you a home then it must provide you with its reasons in writing.[12]

What kind of housing the council will provide

Although government guidelines say that homeless people should be found a permanent home as soon as possible, many councils put them into emergency or temporary accommodation first. This can be a room in a cheap bed and breakfast hotel, a hostel or a house waiting to be improved or demolished. Sometimes people have to stay for several months, or in the worst cases years, in bad conditions in 'temporary' accommodation. Sometimes, for example in a bed and breakfast hotel, you may not be able to take your furniture with you. If you cannot afford to store it and there is therefore a risk of it getting lost or damaged the council must make sure it is stored in a safe place. They can make a reasonable charge for the temporary accommodation and for the furniture storage.[13]

If the council has a duty to find you a permanent home you will eventually be offered somewhere. This will usually, but not always, be a council house or flat. However, councils often offer their least popular types of homes to people who have been homeless and often make only one offer.

If you turn down this offer the council might then decide that it has discharged its duty towards you and has no further obligation to you.

Challenging the council's decision

The Housing Act 1985 imposes legal duties on local councils and gives homeless people legal rights. If you disagree with the council's decision, you might be able to challenge it if you believe that the council has:

- misinterpreted the law, **or**
- reached a grossly unreasonable decision, **or**
- not taken proper account of all the facts.

If you want to challenge the decision it is essential to get good advice as soon as possible. A good advice agency should be able to help you challenge the council's decision and, as a last resort, may be able to advise you how to get legal help to take the council to court.

OTHER RIGHTS TO REHOUSING

In addition to the rights of certain homeless people to housing, people who lose their homes as a result of action by the local council will usually have a right to rehousing.[14] There are a number of circumstances in which people can lose their homes because of council action. For example, the council might make a compulsory purchase order on the house and then demolish it, either because it is in bad condition or because the council wants to use the land for other purposes. The council might decide the property has to be improved and this could mean that the tenants have to move out permanently. The right to rehousing does not apply, however, if the occupiers have to move out only temporarily. Anyone who is lawfully living in the property at the time the council starts its action is eligible for rehousing, so this right applies to owners and tenants. It does not apply to squatters or to people who move in after the council has started its action. Although in practice people rehoused in these circumstances are usually offered some of the best types of housing, the council need offer only temporary accommodation at first and can expect people to wait for an offer of a permanent home.

People who do lose their homes in this way may also claim from the council:[15]

- *A home loss payment* equal to ten times the rateable value of the property. There is a minimum payment of £1,200 and a maximum of £1,500. In order to qualify the owner or tenant must have lived there for five years.

- *A disturbance payment* to help with the costs of moving and setting up a new home. This covers the cost, for example, of removals, reconnections and adjusting curtains and carpets. In order to qualify you must have been living there before the demolition or improvement programme was announced.

- *A well maintained payment:* If the property has been compulsorily purchased by the local council or has had a demolition or closing order on it (see page 121) and if the property has been well maintained, an additional sum is payable to anyone who has undertaken that maintenance, including tenants.[16]

There are additional payments available only to owner occupiers (see page 86).

OTHER COUNCIL HOUSING SCHEMES

In addition to the schemes already described, councils often run special schemes for letting houses and flats. The most usual are:

- *Hard-to-let schemes:* Where the council has unpopular homes (for example, flats in older estates or tower blocks) which are often refused by ordinary applicants, they may be offered to people who would not normally qualify for housing. So, for example, they may be offered to young single people and flat sharers.

- *Key worker schemes:* Some councils will offer homes to so-called 'key workers'. These are people whom they wish to keep in the area because of the type of work they do, particularly if they have skills which are in short supply in that area. Ask the council and also your employer if there are any such schemes in your area.

- *Schemes for special groups:* Some councils have a quota for particular groups whom they want to encourage to stay in the area. For example, some have special schemes for sons and daughters of existing council tenants, or for engaged or newly married couples. Some also have schemes for groups of people with special needs, such as people recovering from a mental illness or ex-offenders.

There are many different kinds of schemes run by different councils, but the numbers of lettings involved are usually small. When you apply to the council for a home, ask for details of any special schemes it runs.

The elderly

Apart from letting ordinary homes to the elderly, local councils also make special provision for them. Most elderly people can lead fully independent lives, but some need extra help without needing the full care of a residential old people's home. For these people, local councils provide sheltered housing. Sheltered housing may be blocks of separate flats or small estates of bungalows. They are usually unfurnished, self-contained and fitted with special features, for example an alarm to call a resident warden in emergencies. Residents' privacy is preserved but social events may be organised for those who wish to participate. As with other types of council housing there is, in many areas, a shortage of places in sheltered housing. Each council decides for itself who should get priority.

THE COUNCIL'S OFFER OF A HOME

The type and quality of council housing varies widely. Some types of property are much more popular than others. Many more people want to live in a house with a garden than in a tower block on a large estate. In many areas, particularly the inner cities, there is a severe shortage of the more popular types of home and the council has to decide who should be offered the different types of property. Families with children are more likely to be offered houses with gardens and ground floor flats. Elderly people may also be offered ground floor or first floor flats. Fit people without children may only have the option of a high-rise flat. But many councils also distinguish between homeless people, who may get only the worst properties, and existing council tenants who are transferring who may get the best, with people from the housing list coming somewhere in between.

Councils also vary in the number of offers they are prepared to make. Some will only make one offer to homeless people. Some limit people from the waiting list to, for example, three offers. There may be a choice of three at once or they may only receive a second offer after turning down the first one.

Some councils may ask you to state your preference when you first register with them, others may wait until they are in a position to make you an offer. It is important to discuss your preferences with the council and to make sure the officer you talk to understands the reasons for your particular preferences. You may, for example, need to live in a particular area for work or family reasons. The more limited you are in the areas or types of property you are prepared to accept the longer you are likely to have to wait. There may be certain areas or property types for which the council will refuse to consider you. It is generally very difficult to get a council to bend these rules unless there is something very unusual about your circumstances, for example very strong medical reasons why you have to live in a ground floor flat.

It is also important to find out how many offers you will be made. However, if you are entitled to three offers the second and third ones will not necessarily be any better than the first. You may be able to get an extra offer if you can show that the one made to you is grossly unsuitable or even a mistake; for example if the council agreed to make you an offer in one area but then failed to. If you are thinking about refusing an offer, always discuss it fully with the council officer who made the offer and explain your reasons why you think it is unsuitable. The home you are offered may fall well short of what you hoped for, but if it is the usual type of property the council offers to people in your circumstances there is likely to be little you can do in the short term to get a better property.

The council will normally give you a chance to look at the property before deciding. If it appears to be in bad condition look closely to find out the reasons. If it needs redecoration the council may agree to do this before you move in or may give you an allowance to do the redecorating yourself. If, however, there are more serious faults you should ask the council to do the necessary repairs before you move in. If they refuse get advice from an independent agency (see Chapter 7). The council has legal obligations to do repairs (see page 133) and an independent advice centre may be able to help you to get the council to do the repairs or to negotiate for an offer of another tenancy.

The council should also tell you how much the rent will be. This is usually payable weekly. On top of the rent you also have to pay rates for the provision of local council services such as refuse collection and schools. The council should tell you how much these rates are and you will normally pay them weekly along with the rent. Many council tenants receive help with their rent and rate payments through the housing benefit scheme. See page 103 for details of the scheme.

Finally, the council should provide you with a written tenancy agreement and an explanation of it.[17] This agreement sets out the rights and duties of both landlord and tenant. It should include details of the landlord's duties to do repairs. These agreements are normally in a standard form, so there is little or no scope for individuals to change any of the terms of the agreement, but if there are things in it you do not like (for example, if you think the council is making you responsible for too many of the repairs) contact a local tenants' association or advice centre as you may, together with other tenants, be able to renegotiate the agreement or even challenge it in the courts if it does not abide by the law.

MOVING TO ANOTHER COUNCIL HOUSE

If you are already a council tenant and want to move to another council property there are a number of ways of doing this.

Transfers

If you want to move within the area of your local council you can apply for a transfer. There are often many more people wishing to transfer than there are suitable properties available. Each council decides for itself who gets priority and some have very long lists of people wanting a transfer. If you have an urgent need to move (for example for serious medical reasons or because you are overcrowded) you are more likely to get priority. Some councils also have arrangements for urgent transfers for people suffering from racial harassment. The council might also give you priority if there is a high demand for the type of property you are living in, if for example you want to transfer from a larger to a smaller home. However, if your present home is adequate but you want to transfer to one of the more popular properties, you may find it difficult or impossible to do so. The council should provide you with written details of how it decides who gets priority for transfers.[18]

Exchanges

Public sector tenants, including secure council and housing association tenants, now have a legal right to exchange their home with other tenants either within their own council's area or in another area.[19] You must get your landlord's permission to do this but the landlord is only allowed to withhold permission for certain limited reasons and must in any event give you an answer within six weeks.

Your landlord or the landlord of the person you want to exchange with can only refuse to allow the exchange for one of the following reasons:

- your landlord has a court order to evict you;
- your landlord has given a notice of proceedings for possession or has started court proceedings giving one of the 'grounds for possession' numbered 1-6 on page 83;
- the accommodation you want to transfer to is substantially larger than you need;
- the accommodation you want to transfer to is too small for your needs;
- the tenant has a job and accommodation in the grounds of a building not mainly used for housing purposes;
- the landlord is a charity and the proposed new tenant is not the type of person who qualifies for help from that charity;
- the accommodation is specially adapted for a person with physical disabilities and the proposed new tenant does not have disabilities;
- the landlord is a housing association or trust which lets only to certain groups of people in need and the proposed new tenant does not fit into one of these groups;
- the accommodation is one of a group of properties normally let to people with special needs, there are special facilities nearby for these people and the proposed new tenant does not need that type of special accommodation;
- the accommodation is managed by a tenants' management co-operative and the proposed tenant is not willing to become a member of the co-operative.

You are not allowed to give or receive any money as a part of the exchange. If you do, both you and the other tenant could be evicted (see page 83). Exchanges can be a useful way of moving areas, but they are rarely a way of getting better quality housing as very few people are prepared to exchange their home for one of lower quality.

There are a number of ways of finding another tenant to exchange with you:

- *The Tenants' Exchange Scheme:* This is a government-supported scheme to put you in touch with tenants in other areas who want to move. You can get an application form from your local council or citizens advice bureau or direct from the Tenants' Exchange Scheme (see *Useful addresses*). The scheme publishes monthly lists of people wanting to move which you can look at in your local housing department. You can then contact suitable tenants directly. The scheme is free of charge.

- *The Mutual Exchange Bureau:* The Mutual Exchange Bureau keeps a register of people wanting to move into, out of or within London. There is no charge for using the service (see *Useful addresses*).

- Ask your *local council* and the council for the area to which you want to move whether they keep lists of people wanting to exchange.

- *Advertise* in local papers in your own area and the area to which you want to move. Weekly papers such as *Exchange and Mart, London Weekly Advertiser* and *Dalton's Weekly* carry advertisements from tenants wishing to exchange. You can also try advertising in local shop windows (especially newsagents) in the area to which you want to move.

The National Mobility Scheme

Tenants of public landlords (including councils, housing associations and new towns), people with high priority on their council's housing list and others with a pressing need to move can apply to their local council to move through the National Mobility Scheme. You need to be able to demonstrate that you have either a *job reason* (that is, you have a job or an offer of employment in the area you want to move to) or a *social reason* (for example, you are elderly and want to live near to relatives). To apply, go to your local council or new town housing department where, if you are eligible, you will be given an application form to fill in. Take any documents that might help your case, such as written confirmation of a job offer. You should be informed on the progress of your application by the authority which receives your nomination. If you have not heard anything after about six weeks, check with your own council. Most housing authorities participate in the scheme but they do so voluntarily and if your application is refused there is little you can do to reverse the decision.

County and London mobility schemes
If you want to move within the county you live in or within London, there are also local mobility schemes. Your local council can give you details.

Council key worker schemes
These are often open to people who live outside the area (see page 22 for details of these schemes).

MOVING TO A NEW TOWN

New towns are designed to offer the opportunity, particularly to inner city residents, to move to new and better houses and environments. These opportunities have declined in recent years but, although fewer people are now able to move, it is still possible to do so. The map on page 184 shows where the new towns are. There are two main ways of moving:

- by taking up employment in the new town;
- by getting a special allocation from the small number available to retired people, one parent families, people with disabilities and retiring members of the armed forces.

The opportunities in both cases are limited and the procedures vary in each different town. You should get further information from the towns in which you are interested. Their offices are listed under *Useful addresses.*

You can also move to the new towns under the other mobility schemes described in this section.

Renting from a private landlord

Private rented homes are increasingly hard to find. They often offer bad value for money, with poor conditions, little security and high rents. However, if you cannot afford to buy, do not qualify for a council or housing association home or only want somewhere temporary, you may have to look for a private rented home. Many landlords will not take certain types of tenant; for example, they may not consider you if you are unemployed or if you have children. Some landlords and accommodation agencies also discriminate against black people. Racial discrimination is generally illegal; if you have suffered from it see page 46.

WHERE TO LOOK

Many people find a home to rent through personal contacts, so it is worth asking friends, family and work colleagues if they know of any places on offer. Landlords also advertise in shop windows and in daily and weekly papers and magazines. Tenants wishing to share with others also often advertise. Because of the shortage of places to rent they are often let very quickly, so it is important to get the papers and magazines as soon as they are published, to telephone any suitable places immediately and to be prepared to visit them the same day.

At the same time you can try accommodation agencies. These often advertise in the same places as landlords and they are also listed in the Yellow Pages telephone directory. Most agencies make a charge, but they are only allowed to do so in law if you actually find and rent a home through the agency.[20] It is illegal for an agency to make any charge if all they do is register your details or supply you with addresses of accommodation which you do not take up. Agencies are not allowed to ask you to pay a deposit which is returnable if no accommodation is found. Most agencies charge a fee of between one and two weeks' rent plus VAT.

An agency is allowed to charge for extra services provided, but only if this was done with your agreement or at your request. For example, an agency could charge if you ask them to negotiate on the tenancy agreement with your prospective landlord. This charge would be payable whether or not you finally get accommodation through the agency. Always ask what other charges might be involved when you first contact the agency. If you believe you should not have been charged or have been overcharged, get advice.

Most agencies will want you to visit them to register. They will probably ask for details of your job and many will not register people who are unemployed. They may want references from your employer, bank or a previous landlord. If they cannot offer you anything immediately, ring them at least once a day to ask if they have any places on their books.

NEGOTIATING THE TENANCY AGREEMENT

As landlords can usually pick and choose between a number of possible tenants it is often difficult to try to bargain over the rent or the tenancy agreement. If you try to do so you may risk losing the offer. However, these are the most important points to look out for:

- Read carefully any *agreement* you are asked to sign and if possible get advice on it before signing.

- Check on the *type of letting* which is being offered and how much security it gives you (see Chapter 2). In many areas most places on offer are only short-term lettings.

- ○ Check on the *rent.* Does it include rates or are these extra? Does it include payments for gas, electricity and services or are these extra?
- ○ Check on how much you have to *pay in advance.* Typically you may have to pay one month's rent in advance and a *deposit* of between one week's and two months' rent.
- ○ Check if there are any other *extra charges.*
- ○ Check on your obligations to repair and decorate the property.
- ○ Check on the other obligations and rights of landlord and tenant that are written into the agreement.

In addition to the tenancy agreement you should also agree with the landlord a written list of any furniture provided by the landlord. This is known as an *'inventory'* and is important in case there is any dispute over the furniture in the future.

You will need to assess how far you feel you can negotiate with the landlord before signing an agreement. In areas of housing shortage where many tenants might be chasing one flat you are obviously in a very weak bargaining position. But remember that the tenancy agreement cannot take away from you any of the rights given to you by the law in Acts of Parliament and described in this guide. Even if you have signed an agreement which says otherwise, you still have these rights.

If you are already a fully protected tenant (see page 50) and the landlord suggests any changes in your tenancy agreement, always get advice before agreeing to them because they could seriously affect your rights.

Renting from a housing association

Housing associations and housing trusts are non-profit-making, independent organisations. They vary in size from associations that own one house to those that have several thousand. Many receive money from the government and from local councils and are registered with the Housing Corporation, a government body which regulates them. They vary widely in the types of people they house. Some operate rather like local councils catering for all types of people and giving priority to those with the most urgent need for housing. Others specialise in helping particular groups of people, for example the elderly, people with disabilities or those with other special needs.

If you want to apply to rent a home from a housing association you can find out from the local council which associations are operating in the area in which you want to live. Many associations take nominations from the local council, so you should ask your council whether it can nominate you. If the council cannot do so, contact the associations and ask them how you can apply. Each association has its own method of assessing applications and deciding who should be offered a home. Housing associations which are registered with the Housing Corporation are obliged by law to provide information on how they allocate their tenancies.[21] Some will take applications directly, others will only take nominations through local agencies such as advice centres or social services. Ask the associations if any local agencies can nominate you. Each agency will have very few nominations, however, so they may not be able to help you. Many associations already have a backlog of applicants. Some keep waiting lists although they may close these to new applicants if they get too long. Others only accept applicants when they have a home ready to offer. Because they vary so widely, it is necessary to contact each association that you are interested in to find out how they operate and whether you have any chance of renting a home through them.

MOVING TO ANOTHER AREA

There are a number of ways in which housing association tenants can move to another area:

- The National Mobility Scheme (see page 26).
- Arrange an exchange (see page 24).
- The Housing Association Liaison Project (HALO). Tenants of housing associations can apply to move through this scheme. Details are available from your housing association.

Renting from a housing co-operative

Housing co-operatives are groups of people who collectively manage and usually own their own housing. They are democratically run so that everyone in the co-op has an equal say in how it is managed. Some co-operatives are based in temporary short life housing (see page 45), others provide permanent homes.

Living in a co-op means greater control for tenants over their own homes, but also a greater commitment of time and energy to managing your own housing. This often means doing unpaid work in your own time such as attending meetings, helping with administration and decorating and repair work. Some of the larger co-ops have elected committees and even employ people to do some of the work, but smaller co-ops often expect all members to do their own share.

The members of the co-op usually consist of the tenants and people waiting to become tenants. As co-ops are a new development in this country there are still only a few in existence and most of these are not open to new members. Your local housing aid centre, housing department or citizens advice bureau should be able to tell you of any co-ops operating in your area.

SETTING UP YOUR OWN CO-OP

If you are interested in setting up your own co-op you will need to get together a group of people who are prepared to put in a lot of hard work and who are committed to a co-operative style of working. Government funds are available to help set up co-ops for people who are in housing need. There are two main types of co-op:

- *Management co-ops* where the tenants have responsibility for some or all of the management of their homes but the ownership remains with the local council or a housing association.

- *Non-equity co-ops* where the tenants themselves collectively own the property but do not have any individual financial stake.

For information on how to go about setting up a co-operative contact the National Federation of Housing Co-ops (see *Useful addresses*).

Buying a home

Home ownership has become increasingly popular in recent years and is encouraged by the government with large subsidies. For many people it offers the best opportunity of getting the home of their choice. But it generally involves higher costs in the early years and problems can arise if you suffer a drop in income, perhaps through losing your job, marriage break-up or retirement. It can then be difficult to keep up mortgage payments and to pay for repairs, so you need to feel sure about the security of your present level of income before deciding to buy.

GETTING A MORTGAGE LOAN

Most people who buy a home do so by taking out a loan for all or part of the cost. Interest is charged on the money loaned and repayments are made to the lender at monthly intervals, usually over a period of 20-25 years. The property is security for the money loaned, so that if the monthly repayments are not made the lenders can take possession of the property and sell it to recover their money. The main sources of loans are building societies and banks. At present loans are in plentiful supply and it is worth shopping around to find the best buy.

- *Building societies* can lend to any home buyer. However, when funds are in short supply people already saving with the society will be given preference. Building societies differ in how much they are prepared to lend and also in the types of property on which they are willing to lend. For example, some societies may be wary of lending on a flat on an upper floor where there is no lift in the block.

  If they decide to offer you a loan the building society will value the property you are planning to buy. The loan you will get is based on this valuation, **not** on the price you actually pay (although, of course, the two might be the same). Building societies will generally lend up to 90 per cent or 95 per cent of their valuation, although it is sometimes possible to get 100 per cent.

  Building societies aim to help their customers, but if you are unhappy with any decision of the branch of your building society, for example on the amount of money they will lend or the type of property they will accept, you should take the matter up with the branch manager and, if still unsatisfied, with the society's head office who may be prepared to reverse the decision.

- *Banks* also offer loans. They operate in a similar way to building societies in terms of how much they will lend and their interests rates are also similar. You should, however, stick to the major high street banks and avoid the smaller fringe banks. Some of the smaller banks charge very high rates of interest and may be more likely to evict you if you fall behind with mortgage repayments.

- *Local councils* can offer mortgages but as their funds are very limited loans are usually only available to council tenants buying their own homes.

There are in addition other sources of loans. However, many of these should be approached with caution. You should get independent advice before agreeing to a loan from one of these sources.

- *Mortgage brokers:* Do not go to a mortgage broker or a firm which offers to find you a mortgage unless you have been unable to get one directly from a building society, bank or local council. Mortgage brokers earn their living by charging commission or fees for arranging mortgages. This commission is earned in one of two ways. First, they can arrange an *'endowment mortgage'* and receive a commission from the insurance company who issue the endowment policy. However, an endowment mortgage may be more expensive and less advantageous for you (see page 35 for the pros and cons of endowment mortgages). Second, the broker may arrange an ordinary building society or bank mortgage. However, you will have to pay the broker a fee for doing this — usually between two and four per cent of the amount of the loan.

  A reliable broker should be registered with the Corporation of Mortgage Brokers and Finance Brokers or with the British Insurance Brokers Association. If a broker is unable to arrange a mortgage for you, then any fee you have paid should be refunded. However, the broker is entitled to charge for any valuations of properties carried out on your behalf.

- *Insurance companies* can arrange endowment mortgages but usually only deal directly in loans for expensive properties at the upper end of the market.

- *Your employer* may be able to arrange a mortgage for you, either from their own funds, which can sometimes be at lower rates of interest, or through links with building societies or banks. However, if you get a loan at a low rate of interest, remember that if you leave that employer you will have to start paying a normal rate of interest which could be difficult if you have borrowed a large amount.

- *Builders* of new homes may arrange special loans from a building society to help with the sale of the properties.

- *Estate agents* can often arrange a mortgage for customers but check whether they are offering an endowment or a standard repayment mortgage (see page 34).

- *Finance companies and small banks:* It is not advisable for anyone to borrow from a finance company for house purchase. They tend to charge very high interest rates and to be readier to evict people who fall behind with repaymens. If you are thinking about borrowing from a finance company or small bank, get independent advice before signing any agreement. If you have already signed an agreement and are having second thoughts, get advice.

HOW MUCH YOU CAN BORROW

All lenders calculate how much they are prepared to lend on the basis of your income. The calculations are based on *gross income*, that is, before any deductions for tax. A proportion of guaranteed overtime payments or bonuses may also be taken into account. Different lenders use different methods of calculation to work out how much they will offer. For example, if there is a couple who are both working, one building society might take 2½ times the higher annual income plus 1¼ times the lower income. So if a couple were earning £6,000 and £4,000 a year, they would take:

2½×£6,000 =	£15,000
1¼×£4,000 =	£ 5,000
Total	£20,000

Another building society might offer 2¾ times the higher income and half the lower. So the same couple would get:

2¾×£6,000 =	£16,500
½×£4,000 =	£ 2,000
Total	£18,500

Under the Sex Discrimination Act 1975 it is illegal for lenders to discriminate against a woman by refusing to use her income as the higher one in their calculations if she is earning more than her partner. Lenders are also not allowed to discriminate against a single woman by offering her less than they would a single man earning the same amount (see page 49).

WHICH TYPE OF MORTGAGE TO CHOOSE

There are two main types of mortgage repayment scheme and you will need to choose which suits you best.

- *Standard repayment mortgages/annuity mortgages:* This type of mortgage is available from building societies, banks and local councils. The monthly repayments are made up of the interest you pay on the amount borrowed and repayment of the loan itself (known as the *capital*). In the first year most of the monthly repayment consists of interest on the loan with only a small amount of capital paid off. But as each year goes by you pay off more of the capital and the interest payments decrease. Provided the interest rate does not change, the repayments stay the same throughout the period of the loan. It is possible with some building societies to arrange for a *low start mortgage.* With these the monthly repayments start off lower than with standard repayments and then begin to increase after a few years to balance out the earlier savings. After a time, the repayments become higher than those for an ordinary mortgage. Low start schemes are only advisable for people whose incomes are guaranteed to rise sufficiently to cope with rising payments. For example, a couple with two incomes which then reduces to one income might find it difficult to meet the rising costs.

○ *Endowment mortgages:* These are available through building societies, banks and insurance companies. Mortgage brokers usually offer to arrange endowment mortgages. They are different from standard repayment mortgages because the capital borrowed is not repaid gradually each year but is instead paid in a lump sum at the end of the mortgage term. In order to achieve this you take out an endowment policy with a life assurance company for which you pay monthly premiums. The life assurance company pays out the lump sum at the end of the mortgage term. The whole loan is paid off by the insurance company if you die before the end of the term. There are three main types of endowment policy:

— a *'guaranteed' or 'non-profit' endowment:* with these policies the life assurance company agrees to pay the exact amount of your loan at the end of the term;

— a *'with profits' endowment:* where the life assurance company repays the sum you borrowed at the end of the mortgage term and in addition pays an extra sum which it calls profits, bonuses or dividends. This kind of mortgage offers an in-built savings scheme, but you will have to pay relatively high monthly premiums to get the bonuses and this makes it more expensive than other forms of mortgage;

— a *'low cost' or 'build-up' endowment* where you take out a 'with profits' policy for less than the amount you borrowed. The idea is that your bonuses will build up so that by the end of the term you will have enough to pay the loan with a small amount left over.

○ *Pension mortgages:* These are available for people who are self-employed, or working for a company that does not have a compulsory occupational pension scheme. As with endowment mortgages, you only repay the interest each month to the lender, but you also pay contributions into a pension scheme which will pay out a lump sum at the end of the term (usually after 25 or 30 years) which pays off the amount borrowed and gives you a pension as well. You receive tax relief at your highest rate of tax on the premiums you pay while the accumulating pension fund is not subject to any tax (though this may change). This is a cheap mortgage for people who are high-rate tax payers, although for a basic rate tax payer it may still be more expensive than an ordinary repayment mortgage. Compare this scheme with an ordinary repayment mortgage and a separate pension or savings plan before making a decision.

The main questions you will want to ask in choosing the best type of mortgage are: Which is the cheapest? What happens if you want to move? What if you have difficulty repaying the loan? 'Guaranteed' and 'with profits' endowment mortgages are more expensive than ordinary repayment mortgages and are not recommended. If you want to build up savings it is better to invest in a separate savings scheme and not to tie it to your mortgage. Even so-called 'low cost' endowment mortgages are often more expensive than ordinary repayment mortgages for standard rate taxpayers. Endowment mortgages may also be less flexible if you want to move. If you run into difficulties in making the mortgage payments, then with an ordinary repayment mortgage it is often possible to extend the period of the loan and so reduce your monthly payments. This is not possible with an endowment mortgage.

THE COST OF BUYING A HOME

There is generous financial help available to reduce the cost of paying off a mortgage; indeed, on average, home owners with mortgages receive a greater subsidy than do council or private tenants. (See page 100 for details of these subsidies.)

But mortgage payments are not the only cost you will have to meet. There are a number of other expenses; some are one-off costs when you buy your home, others are recurring costs.

Initial one-off costs include:

- You will need to make up the difference between what the lender will offer you as a mortgage and the price of the property. In addition, if the lender holds a *retention* while the repairs are done, you will need money to cover that. These sums could amount to several thousands of pounds.

- You will have to pay a *fee for the valuation* of the property which the lender carries out. The charges are usually on a sliding scale related to the price of the property. You might have to pay around £40 + VAT for valuation of a £20,000 property. In addition your own *survey* might cost £150-£200 and a full structural survey might cost £300.

- If you employ *your own solicitor* to handle the legal aspects of the purchase you will have to pay fees which may be around one per cent of the purchase price but could be more or less than this (see page 40).

- You will have to pay a fee to the *lender's solicitor,* probably in the region of £80-£90.

- You may have to pay *Land Registry fees.* In many areas of the country all purchases have to be registered with the Land Registry. The fees vary according to the purchase price of the property and whether it has previously been registered. As an example, on a £40,000 property which is already registered, the fee will be £60.

- *Stamp duty* is a tax payable on all properties costing more than £30,000. The duty payable is one per cent of the purchase price.

- *Setting up costs:* these include removal costs, connection fees for gas, electricity and telephone and, if this is your first home, the cost of furniture, carpets and curtains.

Regular expenses include:

- *Rates* are charged annually or twice yearly by the local council to all owners and tenants for the provision of local services. You can arrange to pay them quarterly or monthly if you wish. Find out from the existing owner or the local council what rates are payable. There will also be a charge for water rates made by the local water authority.

- If you buy a leasehold property (this will usually be a flat — see page 38) you will have to pay annual *ground rent.* A typical ground rent would be in the region of £50-£100 a year, but it could be higher.

- If you buy a flat in a block you will usually have to pay *service charges.* Each occupier pays a share of the cost of common services such as cleaning and routine maintenance. Charges of £200 to £600 a year are not uncommon but they could be higher if there are extensive services such as porters, lifts and gardens. Charges increase as the cost of providing the service rises. There is also usually an obligation to pay your share of any major repairs such as reroofing or repairing the outside of the block.

- The lender will require you to have *insurance* on the property against major damage such as fire. The amount you will have to insure is the cost of rebuilding the property, which can be higher than its market value. This insurance generally costs between £1.25 and £1.50 a year for each £1,000 of insurance. If you have a standard repayment mortgage it is also advisable to consider taking out a mortgage protection policy which means that if you die the mortgage is paid off in full (endowment mortgages are automatically insured). For a healthy person the cost is around £2 per month for each £10,000 insured. In addition, it is advisable to insure the contents of your home.

- *Repairs* do not occur at predictable intervals, but can be very expensive when they do come.
- Try to get details from the present owner of the property of *fuel costs.*
- If your move means a longer journey to work you will have higher *travel costs.*

It is advisable to make at least an estimate of all these costs before committing yourself to buying.

THE STEPS TO BUYING A HOME

You should visit the building society or bank where you are hoping to get a loan to ask for agreement in principle that they will offer a mortgage and to find out what their maximum loan to you would be. The next step is to decide what type of property to buy. You can get an idea of what is available in your price range from local newspapers and estate agents. You may need to consider some of the following options:

- *Freehold or leasehold:* Most houses are freehold, almost all flats are leasehold. When you buy a freehold property, you own it outright. When you buy a leasehold property you buy the right to occupy it for a fixed period. In practice, buying a leasehold property with a long lease (for example 99 years) is little different from buying a freehold, as you will probably sell while the lease still has many years to run. However, as the number of years remaining on the lease decreases, you may come across problems in getting a mortgage. For example building societies are unlikely to lend on a lease with less than 50 years left to run. Even if you did manage to buy it, it could be very difficult to resell. If you live in a leasehold home you cannot normally be evicted when the lease runs out. If you live in a leasehold house (but not a flat) you have rights to buy the freehold. (See page 86 for further details.)
- *Vacant or part possession:* If you buy your home with vacant possession, all previous occupants should move out when the purchase is completed. There should be a clause written into the contract of sale stating that vacant possession will be given, so that if the previous occupants do not move you can sue the person who is selling the property.

You may find a relatively cheap home offered with 'part possession'. This means exactly what it says. You are entitled to possession of only part of the property and the rest is let to tenants. The tenants will almost certainly be protected from eviction and have as much legal right to live there as you. Their protection does not change because the property changes hands. The tenancy may not even end on the death of the tenant because another member of the family living there may automatically inherit the tenancy. Most lenders will offer a mortgage only if you are buying with vacant possession. Therefore, even if you succeed in buying a property with tenants living in part of it, you could have difficulty reselling it in the future.

Finding a property

Estate agents in the area of your choice will have lists of available property displayed in their offices and will also send out lists by post free of charge. Estate agents do not charge buyers, it is the seller who pays them. At times when properties are in high demand they can sell very quickly, so it is worth calling at the estate agents or telephoning regularly rather than waiting for the lists to arrive by post. Local newspapers also carry advertisements for properties.

Negotiating the purchase

It may be possible to bargain a little on the price of the property, especially if demand is low and there is a shortage of prospective buyers. However, the reverse is true when demand is high and you may find you have been outbid by someone else. Any written offer from you should state that it is made 'subject to survey and contract' which means that you are not bound to go through with it at this stage. Until you *exchange contracts* (see below) neither seller nor buyer are legally bound. If your offer is accepted you will probably be asked to pay a holding deposit. This could range from £50 to £250, or possibly even more, but it will be deducted from the final purchase price and you should get it back if the sale falls through. You can refuse to pay it, but if you decide to agree you should get a receipt for the deposit and make sure that it states that the estate agent or solicitor who is holding the deposit does so 'as stake-holder'.

Applying for a mortgage

As soon as you have agreed a price for the property you should apply for a mortgage. (See page 34 for details of the types of mortgage available.) You will have to fill in an application form and pay a fee for the valuation of the property. This valuation is undertaken for the lender by a qualified valuer and some lenders will let you see a copy of the report. It is important to realise that this valuation is **not** a detailed survey of the property and will not necessarily disclose, for example, structural defects which could be very expensive to put right. It is therefore highly advisable to have your own independent structural survey done before going ahead with the purchase. This could cost £150-200 but may save you thousands of pounds later on. It is often possible to save money by combining your lender's valuation survey with your own structural survey; ask your lender if this is possible. Most major building societies now offer a full survey at competitive cost.

If the valuation report reveals that some repairs or improvements are necessary to the property, part of the loan may be withheld until these works are done satisfactorily. This is called a *retention.* As you cannot normally do the work before completing your purchase, you will need extra cash to make up the amount retained. The actual cost of the work may be higher than the amount of the retention, so make sure you can afford it by getting builders' estimates for the work. You may qualify for a grant from the local council to help pay for part of the cost (see page 138).

In addition to checking on the property, the lenders will check on your financial position. They will write to your employers to check on your income and possibly to your bank or landlord for a reference. If you are self-employed you will have to provide tax returns and accounts covering the past two or three years as proof of your income.

The legal steps

Most people use a solicitor to deal with the legal side of buying a home. This involves making enquiries to check whether anyone else has any claims to or rights over the property, whether services such as electricity, gas and water are connected to the property and whether there are any problems with the local council over planning permission. This process is known as *conveyancing.*

It is possible to do the conveyancing yourself although the seller's solicitor may be unhelpful if you do so. But if you are used to doing paperwork and do not feel intimidated by legal jargon or by solicitors you can save several hundred pounds. It is not nearly so complicated as most solicitors like to pretend. This is particularly so for freehold properties. Leaseholds are more complicated and you would need to get legal advice over the lease.

If you decide to do it yourself there are several guides available (see *Useful publications).* If, like most people, you decide to use a solicitor there are a number of ways you can reduce costs:

- Ask your lender for a recommended solicitor. Your lenders will also use a solicitor to handle their legal work. Ask if you can both use the same solicitor as this will avoid duplicating work and save costs.
- Ask friends for recommendations.

- ○ Ask a number of solicitors for estimates of their costs. Find out whether these costs include VAT and 'disbursements' (that is, costs paid on your behalf by the solicitor).

Once the final price has been agreed, you have a written offer of a mortgage and you or your solicitor have completed all the necessary investigations you are in a position to *exchange contracts.* This simply means that you enter into a legally binding contract to buy the property on a certain date, so you must be sure that you have all the necessary money available and that the legal investigation has been properly completed. Your solicitor will send your signed contract together with a deposit (usually 10 per cent of the purchase price) to the seller's solicitor and will receive a signed contract in return. If you cannot afford the 10 per cent deposit you may be able to negotiate a lower deposit of perhaps five per cent. If the seller will not agree to this you will have to take out a short-term loan to cover it. If you have a bank account, ask to borrow from the bank. Avoid finance companies as their interest rates are very high. Alternatively, it is possible to take out an insurance policy which will pay the vendor if you default on the contract. This can be cheaper than taking out a bridging loan. Ask your solicitor or building society for details.

Once you have exchanged contracts you are legally committed to buy, even if the house burns down before the sale is completed. It is therefore essential that the property is insured by you from the time the contracts are exchanged. The date when you complete the purchase is normally 28 days after the exchange of contracts, although this can be varied.

LOW COST HOME OWNERSHIP SCHEMES

There are a number of low cost schemes to help people who might not otherwise be able to buy their own homes.

Shared ownership schemes

These schemes are run by some local councils, new towns and housing associations. You take out a loan to buy a share in the value of the property (typically between 25 and 90 per cent) and pay rent on the remaining share. Under most schemes you have a legal right to buy out the remaining share held by your landlords either in stages or all in one go.

Although these schemes are designed for people who cannot afford the full cost of ownership, they can sometimes work out no cheaper than taking out a full loan on an older or smaller property. Check on property prices in the area to make sure there is nothing suitable in your price range. Even though you own only part of the property you will normally have the full responsibility for repairs and maintenance. You should check that you will be able to afford the cost of this. If you are interested in shared ownership you can get details from local councils and new town development corporations in the areas you would like to live in. You can get details of housing association schemes from the Housing Corporation (see *Useful addresses*).

Leasehold for the elderly

Some housing associations run special schemes to provide sheltered housing for elderly people. You pay 70 or 80 per cent of the cost of the property and the rest is made up by government grant. When leaseholders leave or die they or their beneficiaries receive 70 or 80 per cent of the current market value of the property. Your local council should be able to give you the details of housing associations operating these schemes in your area.

Rental purchase

Rental purchase schemes are operated by private owners. The idea is that you make payments towards the purchase of a property but, unlike someone who has a mortgage, you do not actually own the property until you have paid off all the agreed costs.

Although some of these schemes are genuine, many are simply devices to rent out property without giving you the legal protection which ordinary tenants have. If you are offered an agreement like this, get advice before signing anything.

Rental purchasers are considered in law as *licensees* and as such have very limited legal rights (see page 51). Like other licensees, you can try to argue that your agreement is a sham and simply a device to deprive you of the legal protection you would have as a tenant. Even if the rental purchase agreement is genuine, you do have some protection. If the owners want to evict you they have to go to court to ask for a possession order and the court has wide powers to postpone or suspend any order. It is a criminal offence to evict a rental purchaser without a possession order.[22]

Homesteading

Under homesteading schemes, which are run by some local councils, you buy a run-down property and your mortgage payments are deferred for a few years to enable you to pay for the work required to put it into good condition. For example, some councils defer the start of the mortgage payments for three years. Obviously, the cost of the property will be relatively low as it will be in bad condition. However, remember that putting the property into good condition is likely to cost several thousand pounds unless you can do a large amount of the work yourself.

Other low cost home ownership schemes

Some local councils and housing associations have other schemes to offer lower cost homes to people who could not otherwise afford to buy. For example, some buy and improve older properties and then resell them. Some also have arrangements with private developers to provide low cost 'starter' homes for first-time buyers. Ask your local council and any housing associations in your area.

Temporary and emergency housing

If you find yourself with nowhere to live and the council does not have a responsibility to provide you with housing you may have to find short-term emergency accommodation (see page 16 for details of the help councils must give to homeless people). This section gives details of the emergency and temporary housing that is available. Some *hostels* aim to take people in emergencies, others cater for longer-term stays. *Bed and breakfast hotels* are always available if you can afford the prices, but no one would want to stay in one for long. Some people resort in desperation to *squatting*. Finally, there are groups which provide *short life housing*, but this is not usually available in an emergency.

HOSTELS

Hostels vary widely in the type and quality of accommodation they provide, in what they charge, in the types of people they are prepared to accept and in how long they allow people to stay. They fall into three main groups:

- *Emergency hostels:* These are for people who are homeless and have nowhere to stay that night. Some will take people with no money. Many are of a very low standard with beds in dormitories or cubicles and with large numbers of people sharing washing and toilet facilities. The best ones are decent and well-run but still spartan. You are often only allowed to stay for a short period, perhaps just for a few days.

- *Longer-term hostels:* These are for longer stays. Standards and prices vary enormously. Some are for particular groups, for example students or working women. Many will only take people of certain ages. Some provide meals, others have facilities to cook for yourself.

- *Supportive and therapeutic hostels:* These are for people with particular problems, who need some degree of support. Some are for temporary stays, for example hostels for people receiving treatment for addiction to drink or drugs or for psychiatric illness. Some provide long-term supportive homes, for example for people suffering from mental or physical handicaps.

For help with the cost of living in a hostel see page 113. To find a hostel in your area contact local advice agencies and the housing department and social services department of the local council.

WOMEN'S REFUGES

Women who have to leave home because of violence or threats of violence can try to get a place in a women's refuge. These provide shelter, advice and emotional support for battered women and their children if they have any. You do not have to have any money and you will be helped to claim social security if you qualify. Because women's refuges do not like to turn people away, they can sometimes be crowded but they will always try to take you in in an emergency and try to help you find somewhere to live in the longer term. You do not have to go to a refuge in the area in which you normally live. The Women's Aid Federation England (WAFE) have an emergency 24 hour telephone service if you need to find somewhere (see *Useful addresses*).

BED AND BREAKFAST HOTELS

Even the cheapest hotels are more expensive than many hostels and they often have very poor standards. You will usually have to pay in advance and may have to share a room if you cannot afford very much. If you are homeless and on social security you may be able to get help to pay some or all of the cost (see page 113).

For details of cheap bed and breakfast hotels in your area contact local advice agencies.

SQUATTING

Some homeless people are forced to squat because they cannot find anywhere else to live. Squatters are people who enter into and stay in property without the permission of the owner. They can be evicted very rapidly (see page 89) but squatting is not in itself a crime. However, if you break into a property to squat you risk committing an offence if you damage the doors or windows, however slightly.

Some squatters are able to stay for several months, others are evicted after a few weeks or even days. In some circumstances you might have to leave as soon as you are asked to do so (see page 90). You should look at all other ways of solving your housing problem before deciding to squat.

If you decide that squatting is your only option, there are a few basic rules to observe in order to avoid breaking the law:

- **Never** squat a property that looks as if it might be lived in.
- **Do not break in** if you can avoid it. It you are caught you could be charged with committing criminal damage. If you do break anything mend it as soon as possible.
- Try to find a place which has been empty for some time.
- If a bailiff comes with a warrant to evict you, do not obstruct him or her or refuse to leave.
- Do not use the gas or electricity supplies without making proper arrangements with the appropriate fuel board. If you do so you could be charged with theft.

If you are thinking about squatting it is much better to do it through an organised group than on your own. For advice and details of local groups contact the Advisory Service for Squatters (see *Useful addresses*) and read the *Squatters' Handbook* (see *Useful publications*).

SHORT LIFE HOUSING

The idea of short life housing is to make use of houses that are waiting to be repaired, improved or demolished rather than leaving them standing empty. The properties that are used in this way are usually owned by local councils or housing associations. Most commonly, a group of people take over the houses for a limited period and patch them up to make them habitable. The period varies — it can be as short as a few months or as long as five or more years. In most cases the occupiers do not have security and have to leave when the landlord wants the property back. There is often no guarantee of alternative housing at the end of the period.

Most short life housing groups only take people without children. Many are organised as tenants' co-operatives (see page 30). In these, you will be expected to play a full part in running the group, going to meetings and helping with repair work. There is usually a waiting list for housing and many do not take new members. For details of local short life groups contact your local advice agency.

You might decide to set up your own group. You will need dedicated people who are willing to work hard to set up the group and get the agreement of a local council or housing association to let you have properties. For advice on setting up your own group contact the Empty Property Unit (see *Useful addresses*).

Race and sex discrimination

RACIAL DISCRIMINATION

Black and other ethnic minority people often suffer from discrimination in their search for a home. There is clear evidence of discrimination by some landlords, accommodation agencies and estate agents. Much of this is against the law. This section describes the law as set out in the Race Relations Act 1976 and tells you what to do if you encounter illegal discrimination.

What is discrimination?

The Race Relations Act defines three types of discrimination:[23]

- *Direct discrimination* means treating someone less favourably than others because of their race.

- *Indirect discrimination* means applying a rule which cannot be justified on non-racial grounds and which, whether intentionally or not, has a disproportionately adverse effect on a particular racial group. So, for example, it would be indirect discrimination for a landlord to say that he or she would not take any tenant who cooked curry.

- *Victimisation* means treating one person less favourably than another because he or she has made a complaint or given information about alleged illegal racial discrimination.

Discrimination by accommodation agencies and landlords[24]

It is illegal for *accommodation agencies* to discriminate either directly or indirectly against anyone seeking accommodation by:

- refusing or deliberately omitting to provide details of available accommodation;

- refusing or deliberately omitting to provide their services on the same terms, in the same manner and of the same quality as would normally be provided to other people.

So, for example, even if a landlord tells an accommodation agency that he or she does not want any black tenants, it is still illegal for the agency to follow this instruction and to exclude black applicants.

However, *small premises* are exempt from this provision. See below for the definition of small premises.

It is illegal for *landlords,* both private and public, or anyone acting on behalf of a landlord, to discriminate on racial grounds either directly or indirectly, against people applying to rent accommodation by:

- offering the accommodation on inferior terms;
- refusing an application for a tenancy;
- treating the applicant in any way less favourably than other people in need of such accommodation.

It is also illegal for landlords or tenants to discriminate in the subletting or assigning of tenancies. So, for example, a landlord cannot refuse to let a tenant sublet to a particular person on the grounds of that person's race.[25]

Small premises

Small premises are exempt from these provisions.[26] It is not illegal for a landlord or an accommodation agency to discriminate on racial grounds by the letting of accommodation which counts as small premises. In order to count as small premises **all** of the following must apply:

- the landlord or a near relative (defined as a wife, husband, parent, child, grandparent, grandchild, brother or sister) must live on the premises and intend to continue living there, **and**
- the landlord or near relative must share some of the accommodation with the tenant — this covers bathrooms, kitchens and living rooms but not means of access or storage space, **and**
- there is in addition to the accommodation occupied by the landlord or near relative, accommodation for no more than two other separate households if the property is divided into separate lettings, or for no more than six other people in the case of a boarding house.

Discrimination against existing tenants

It is also illegal for a landlord or anyone managing accommodation to:[27]

- refuse or deliberately omit to give normal benefits and facilities to anyone occupying the premises because of their racial origin;
- evict someone or subject them to inferior treatment because of their racial origin.

This applies to all occupiers even if the accommodation falls within the definition of small premises (see above).

Inducing or helping others to discriminate

It is illegal for a landlord to instruct an accommodation agency or an employee to discriminate on racial grounds. This would include, for example, expressing a 'preference' for tenants of a particular racial group as this is, in effect, treating one group more favourably than another. If a landlord tells an agency that accommodation is exempt from the law because it qualifies as small premises, the agency is not permitted to accept the landlord's word but must take all reasonable steps to check that it does meet all the conditions required to qualify as small premises.

In addition to these specific provisions, the Race Relations Act also places a duty on local authorities to make appropriate arrangements to ensure that their various functions are carried out with due regard to the elimination of unlawful racial discrimination and to the promotion of equality of opportunity and good relations between people of different racial groups.[28]

Estate agents

Estate agents are in the same position as accommodation agencies. It is illegal for them to discriminate against anyone seeking their services by:[29]

- refusing or deliberately omitting to provide their services;
- refusing or deliberately omitting to provide services on the same terms, in the same manner and of the same quality as would normally be provided to other people.

So, for example, it is illegal for an estate agency to accept an instruction from someone wanting to sell their house that they would not consider a black buyer.

However, it is not illegal for someone who is the owner of a property to discriminate if they sell it privately without advertising or using an estate agent.

Action against racial discrimination

Anyone who suffers from illegal racial discrimination by accommodation agencies, landlords or estate agents can take proceedings in the County Court. They can get a declaration of their rights, damages (including damages for injury to feelings) and an injunction or order against the person or agency that has discriminated. Advice and assistance is available from the Commission for Racial Equality, who also have the power to conduct a formal investigation into organisations in order to eliminate discrimination (see *Useful addresses*).

SEX DISCRIMINATION

The Sex Discrimination Act 1975 makes many forms of discrimination against women (or men), on the grounds of their sex, illegal. Because such discrimination usually happens to women this section refers to women, but it is equally applicable to men. The provisions against discrimination over housing are very similar to those of the Race Relations Act. The Sex Discrimination Act covers:[30]

- *Direct discrimination,* meaning treating a woman less favourably than a man simply because she is a woman.
- *Indirect discrimination,* meaning applying a rule which has a disproportionately adverse effect on women.
- *Victimisation,* meaning treating a woman less favourably because she has tried to enforce her rights under the Sex Discrimination Act.

As with racial discrimination (see above) it is illegal to discriminate against women in the sale or letting of property and in the treatment of people occupying accommodation. So, for example, it is illegal for:[31]

- local councils to treat women applicants for housing less favourably than men;
- estate agents and accommodation agencies to discriminate against women;
- landlords to offer female tenants worse facilities than male tenants.

Small premises are, however, exempt as they are under the Race Relations Act (see page 47).

If you apply for a mortgage it is illegal for the building society or bank to treat you less favourably than a male applicant.[32] So, for example, if you apply jointly with a man for a mortgage, building societies must not treat your income less favourably just because you are a woman. Building societies often use a formula such as offering a loan equivalent to 2½ times the higher annual income and 1¼ times the lower income of the couple. If the woman's income is higher, the building society must use her income as the higher one in their calculation and not use the man's income instead.

Action against sex discrimination

People who suffer from sex discrimination can take court action in the same way as those who suffer from racial discrimination. Advice and assistance is available from the Equal Opportunities Commission (see *Useful addresses*).

2: Keeping your home

Private tenants and licensees

All people who rent from a private landlord have some degree of protection from eviction from their homes. But the amount of protection you have varies enormously depending on the arrangements you have made with the landlord and the date when the tenancy began. The provisions relating to protection from eviction are some of the most complex parts of housing law. Pages 52-67 and 72-75 deal with tenancies which began before 15 January 1989. Pages 63 and 67-79 deal with tenancies which began on or after 15 January 1989.

In very broad terms people renting from private landlords fall into one of the following categories:

- The largest group is *tenants of non-resident landlords* (that is landlords who do not live in the same house). These tenants are generally *fully protected* if their tenancy began before 15 January 1989 and it is very difficult for the landlord to evict them as long as they pay the rent and act reasonably. If their tenancy began on or after 15 January 1989 they will usually be assured or shorthold tenants, with less protection.

- The next largest group is *tenants of resident landlords* (that is landlords who live in the same house). In general these tenants have very limited protection. The landlord has a right to evict them but the tenant may be able to delay the eviction for a while.

- There is a smaller group of people renting a home who have very little security because the landlord has arranged the letting so as to remove much of their legal protection. The numbers of these types of lettings are growing. They may be a so-called *holiday let* (whether or not you are on holiday) or a *licence* or a *company let*; with these you have very little protection from eviction.

- There are people who *share their home*, such as flat sharers. Their position is very complicated and depends on the arrangements made with the landlord. Some are fully protected, others have very little protection.

- There are people who live in *tied housing* whose home goes with the job. Generally they have only limited protection.

- There are *agricultural workers* who have special protection and also special rights to rehousing if they are evicted.

- There are new forms of tenancy, so far very few in number, known as *shorthold* and *assured tenancies*.

This section is designed to help you decide:

- what kind of letting you have, and so

- what degree of protection you have.

It is the most complicated section of this guide, but even so gives only an outline of the law. If you are at all unclear about your own position you will need to get expert advice.

TENANT OR LICENSEE?

The first question to answer is whether you are a tenant at all. Just because you make regular payments to the owner of your home you are not automatically a tenant in the eyes of the law. The great majority of people who rent are tenants, but a few people in these circumstances are in fact only *licensees*. It is essential to find out whether you are a tenant or a licensee, because many of the rights given by law apply only to tenants and not to licensees. Unfortunately, although the distinction between the two is of the greatest importance, in practice the dividing line between them can be unclear and borderline cases can only be decided by looking at all the individual circumstances. The difference between them is not defined in any legislation but a recent legal case that went to the House of Lords has clarified the position. Before this case landlords were increasingly using bogus 'licences' to deprive tenants of protection. It is now much more difficult for landlords to do this.

In broad terms a *tenant* is someone who has a legally binding right to occupy a property and to exclude other people from it. A *licensee* is someone who merely has the permission of the owner to be in the property. So, for example, at one extreme someone who visits your house as a guest is your licensee. People living in hostels or staying temporarily in a hotel are usually licensees. Lodgers are one of the most common types of licensee. On the other hand, someone who pays rent on a house or flat for their sole occupation is usually a tenant.

In deciding whether you are a tenant or a licensee the first question is: *is there a written agreement?* Contracts between landlords and tenants or licensees do not have to be in writing. But if there is a written agreement this is the first place to look. Does it mention 'tenant' or 'tenancy', 'licensee' or 'licence'? However, you are not necessarily a licensee just because your landlord has made you sign a piece of paper which describes you as one. If the matter goes to court, the judge should look at all the circumstances surrounding the agreement to make sure it is not merely a sham. The points the court will consider are:

- *Does the occupier have 'exclusive possession' of the accommodation?* This means that the occupier has the exclusive right to live in the premises. Unless you have this right over at least part of the accommodation you cannot be a tenant. One pointer here is whether the accommodation has its own locked door with keys held only by the occupier. If you are forced to share all the accommodation with other people you may well be a licensee. Where people are sharing voluntarily (as with flat sharers) the position is even less clear (see page 73 for further details).

- What were the *true intentions* of the landlord and occupier when they came to their agreement? It is almost certainly a tenancy if there was a letting of self-contained accommodation and you pay rent. If, however, the accommodation is in a hotel or hostel and the owner has unrestricted access to your accommodation you will be a licensee. If the accommodation was provided as an act of friendship or free of charge, you are also likely to be a licensee.

If your landlord claims that you are a licensee but you believe that in reality you are a tenant you can dispute this claim, and, if you win, gain all the rights of a tenant. If you have your own self-contained accommodation and are not a lodger then you are probably a tenant, regardless of any agreement you might have signed. Get advice.

The following sections are for tenants. If you are a licensee, turn to page 75. If your tenancy began on or after 15 January 1989 turn to page 67.

TENANCIES WHICH BEGAN BEFORE 15 JANUARY 1989

The Rent Act 1977 gives varying degrees of protection to most tenancies which began before 15 January 1989. Those that have *full protection* are known as *regulated tenancies*. But some are excluded.

TENANCIES WHICH BEGAN BEFORE 15 JANUARY 1989 BUT WHICH ARE NOT FULLY PROTECTED BY THE RENT ACT 1977

The following types of tenancies are exempt from full Rent Act protection:[1]

- *Homes where the rateable value is very high:* This usually means above £1,500 in Greater London or £750 elsewhere. However, some with higher rateable values may still be protected. In practice only a tiny number of lettings are excluded from protection because they are above these limits.

- *Tenancies where the rent is very low:* Again this affects only a very small number of tenancies, but you may not be protected if you pay no rent or if the annual rent is less than two thirds of the rateable value. This exclusion does **not** apply to former 'controlled' tenancies. (These are tenancies which started before July 1957 where a controlled rent was fixed at a very low level. They were abolished in 1980 and their rents are being brought up to the level of 'fair rents' in regulated tenancies.)

- *Dwellings let with other lands* where the tenancy of the dwelling itself is not the main purpose of the letting.

- Tenancies where the rent includes payment for *board.* 'Board' means the provision of meals, not just a cup of tea. Some landlords try to exclude their tenants from Rent Act protection by providing very limited board. A box of groceries provided every week should not count as board, but a continental breakfast prepared and served on the premises probably would.

  If you make payments for board and the value of the board forms a *substantial* part of the rent then you have only *basic protection* (see page 72 for what this means). If you make payments for genuine board (that is more than just a cup of tea) but these do **not** add up to a substantial part of the rent then you have *restricted protection* (see page 60).

  What is meant by a *substantial part of the rent?* You need to work out the value to you in money terms of the board provided. If this value comes to more than 20 per cent of your rent, it will count as substantial. If it comes to less than 10 per cent it will not count as substantial. If the value is between 10 and 20 per cent the outcome would depend on the decision of the judge if the case came to Court.

  If the landlord is claiming you are not a protected tenant because you receive board, you should get advice.

- Tenancies where the rent includes payment for *a substantial amount of 'attendances'*. Attendances mean personal services to the tenant. They include, for example, cleaning the tenant's own room, but do not include cleaning of common parts of the building or the provision of gas, electricity or hot water. If the value of the attendances provided is substantial (the definition is the same as for substantial board, see above) then you have *restricted protection* (see page 60). If the value of the attendance does **not** form a substantial part of the rent, then they do not affect your security and you remain fully protected.

- *Lettings to students by educational institutions:* The educational institutions which are allowed to let to students without Rent Act protection have to be approved by the Department of the Environment, so ordinary landlords cannot use this as a dodge to get around the Rent Act unless they let to a registered college which then sublets to its students.

- *Holiday lettings:* A tenancy is not protected if the purpose of the letting is that the tenant occupies it for a holiday. This is one of the major loopholes used by landlords to ensure their tenants are not protected. However, a tenancy is not necessarily a holiday let just because you have signed a piece of paper describing it as that. If the tenant argues that this is a sham, the courts must look at the true circumstances of the letting. If there is a written agreement stating it is a holiday let, then the burden is on you to prove that neither you **nor the landlord** intended to create a holiday let. One way to do this would be to prove that the landlord knew you were not on holiday.

- *Agricultural holdings:* These are not protected. However, many agricultural workers in tied housing are protected by the Rent (Agriculture) Act 1976, see page 64.

- *Licensed premises:* Tenancies of dwellings licensed for the sale of alcohol on the premises are not protected.

- *Resident landlords:* The most important exemptions from full Rent Act protection are lettings by resident landlords. To qualify as *resident* the landlord must have lived in the same building as the tenant, continuously since the start of the tenancy. The landlord does not count as resident, however, if the building is a purpose-built block of flats, unless the landlord lives in the same flat as you.

  Since 14 August 1974, all new lettings by resident landlords have been exempt from full protection. However, lettings by resident landlords of *unfurnished* accommodation that began before 14 August 1974 are fully protected (unless they are exempt on some other grounds — for example living accommodation with the landlord). All tenancies where there is a resident landlord which began after 14 August 1974 will normally have only *restricted protection* (see page 60 for what this means).

- *The landlord is the Crown or a government department:* However, tenants of the Crown Estate Commissioners are protected by the Rent Act.
- *Public sector landlords:* Tenants of local councils, housing associations, housing trusts, new towns, the Housing Corporation, housing co-operatives and other public housing bodies have their own legal protection and are not covered by the Rent Act (see page 79).
- *Assured tenancies:* This is a new form of tenancy of which very few exist. They are not regulated (see page 67).
- Lettings where the main purpose of the tenant is to carry on a *business*.[2]
- Lettings where the tenant *shares living accommodation with the landlord.* This means sharing a kitchen or living room — but sharing only a bathroom or WC does not count. Such tenants may have restricted protection (see page 60). Sharing living accommodation with other *tenants* does not automatically reduce your protection.[3]
- Lettings where the tenant is a *company* rather than a person. This is because to qualify for protection tenants must live in the property as their home and a company cannot do this.[4] These so-called 'company lets' are another dodge used by landlords to try to remove protection from their tenants. You may be asked to form a company to rent the property rather than renting it as an individual.
- *Tenancies which lose their Rent Act protection:* A tenancy may have Rent Act protection but then lose it because a closing or demolition order is put on the property by the local council (see page 121),[5] because it is illegally overcrowded (see page 129),[6] or because the tenancy agreement has ended and you are no longer using the premises as your home.

  In addition to these exemptions there is also a form of tenancy known as a *shorthold tenancy*. If you have an agreement which states that you are a shorthold tenant see page 62.

Most ordinary tenants of non-resident private landlords whose tenancy began before 15 January 1989 do not fall into any of these exempted categories and are regulated tenants with full Rent Act protection. They have the right to have a fair rent fixed (see page 91) and to protection

from eviction, and have a wide range of other rights.

The next section describes the rights to protection from eviction of *regulated* tenants with full Rent Act protection.

For details of the rights of:

- tenants of resident landlords with restricted protection, see page 60;
- tenants whose letting began on or after 15 January 1989, see pages 67-79;
- other tenants, see pages 62-66.

REGULATED TENANTS: PROTECTION FROM EVICTION

Regulated tenants can only be evicted on very limited grounds which are set out in law. They do not have to leave just because the landlord gives them notice to quit or because the tenancy agreement has run out. Anyone whose landlord asks them to leave should get advice immediately.

The course of action the landlord must take if he or she wants a tenant to leave depends on the *type* of regulated tenancy that exists.

Is the regulated tenancy 'contractual' or 'statutory'?

Regulated tenancies can be either *contractual* or *statutory*. All tenancies start with some form of agreement between the landlord and the tenant. This agreement is a contract and it can be in writing or merely by word of mouth. This is a contractual tenancy. The contract can be one of two types:

- *a fixed term tenancy,* for example six months or a year; **or**
- *a periodic tenancy* meaning that there is no fixed end to the tenancy and rent is paid periodically, usually either weekly or monthly.

Ending the tenancy

A *fixed term tenancy* comes to an end automatically at the end of the time specified in the agreement. A *periodic tenancy* continues indefinitely from week to week or month to month and the landlord can only bring it to an end if he or she serves a *Notice to Quit* in the proper legal form (see below).

When either a periodic or fixed term tenancy comes to an end the tenant does not have to leave, because it automatically becomes what is known as a *statutory tenancy* . This means that, although the contract between the landlord and tenant has ended, the tenancy still continues on substantially the same terms as before and with the protection of the Rent Act as long as the tenant continues to live there.

Notice to Quit

Where the landlord wants to seek a possession order against a periodic tenant, he or she must first give the tenant a Notice to Quit in the proper legal form.[7] It must be in writing and give at least four weeks' notice or longer if the rent is paid over longer periods. It should expire on a rent day or the day before a rent day. It must also tell the tenants that they do not have to leave unless the landlord gets a court order, and must give information on where to get advice.[8] If the Notice to Quit is not in this form then it has no legal force and the landlord cannot take any further action until a proper notice has been served.

Grounds for eviction

If the tenancy is for a *fixed term* and it has not yet expired the landlord can only go to court for a possession order if the tenant has broken one of the terms of the tenancy agreement and the agreement specifies that the tenancy can be ended for that reason. The landlord must also prove it is reasonable for the court to grant a possession order.

If the tenancy agreement is for an indefinite period (a *periodic tenancy*) the landlord must first bring the tenancy to an end by a Notice to Quit. Once the Notice to Quit has expired and the tenancy has become a *statutory tenancy* (see above) the landlord can try to persuade the court to grant a possession order against the tenant. Any tenant will only have to leave if the court grants an order to the landlord.

To get such an order against a regulated tenant the landlord must prove one of the grounds for possession set out in the Rent Act 1977.[9] The first set of grounds are known as *discretionary cases*. This means that the court **may** grant a possession order but only if the landlord can prove the ground **and** the court thinks that it is *reasonable* to grant an order. The court also has the power to suspend any possession order either for a fixed period, or indefinitely subject to certain conditions — for example the court might make an order for possession because of rent arrears but suspend the order to give the tenant an opportunity to pay off the arrears. Then, as long as the tenant pays off the agreed amounts, the order will not take effect.

The discretionary grounds for possession are:

Case 1 The tenant is in rent arrears or has broken some other term of the tenancy.

Case 2 The tenant or someone else living in the home has caused a nuisance or annoyance to neighbours or has been convicted of using the property for immoral or illegal purposes.

Case 3 The tenant or someone else living in the home has damaged or neglected the property.

Case 4 The tenant or someone living in the home has damaged furniture provided by the landlord.

Case 5 The landlord has made a contract to sell or let the property because the tenant gave notice that he or she was giving up the tenancy.

Case 6 The tenant has assigned or sublet the whole of the property to another person without the landlord's consent. See page 145 for more details of the law governing subletting and assignment.

Case 7 This has been repealed.

Case 8 The tenant was an employee of the landlord, has now left that employment and the landlord reasonably requires the property for a new employee. (For further details of the rights of people whose homes go with their job see page 63.)

Case 9 The property is reasonably required by the landlord as a home for him or herself, for any child over 18, or for parents or parents-in-law. But this case does not normally apply if the landlord purchased the property with tenants already in occupation. The tenant can, as a defence against this case, seek to prove that greater hardship would be caused to the tenant by granting the order than to the landlord by refusing it. In practice, it is very difficult for landlords to use this case as a ground for a possession order.

Case 10 The rent for the property has been fixed by a Rent Officer or Rent Tribunal and the tenant has charged a subtenant more than is allowed under the Rent Act (see page 91 for details of what rents can be charged).

Landlords can also seek possession if they can prove that *suitable alternative accommodation* is available to the tenant.[10] This might be an offer of accommodation from the local council or of another property owned by the landlord. In deciding whether the alternative accommodation offered is suitable the court will take into account the type and size of accommodation, its suitability for the tenant, its distance from work, its cost, the degree of security it offers and its similarity to the present home.[11] The court must consider the accommodation is suitable **and** also consider that it is *reasonable* to grant a possession order. It is not easy for landlords to satisfy courts on both these points.

In all cases where the court has discretion whether or not to grant a possession order (that is, in Cases 1-10 above and in the case of an offer of suitable alternative accommodation), the court may well refuse to grant an order. In Cases 1-10 above the court may grant a suspended order. So, for example, if you can show that you will be able to pay off rent arrears over a reasonable period of time, as long as you stick to this agreement

there is no danger of eviction. So even if one of the discretionary grounds does apply to you it is often worth arguing that it would be unreasonable to grant the order or that it should be suspended.

The second set of grounds for possession are known as *mandatory cases*.[12] This means that, if the landlord can prove that one of these grounds exists, the court **must** grant a possession order and cannot suspend it for more than 14 days unless there would be exceptional hardship, in which case the maximum is six weeks. **In all mandatory cases the landlord must give a written notice at the start of the tenancy (before the grant of the tenancy in Case 19) that the landlord might seek a possession order under that case.**

The mandatory grounds for possession are:

Case 11 The landlord has let his or her own home and intends to return to live there at a future date. This case can also be used if the owner needs to sell with vacant possession to buy a home nearer to a place of work. If the owner dies, a member of the family who was previously living with him or her and who wishes to live there again can also regain possession, either if they want to live in it or if they want to sell it with vacant possession. If there is a mortgage on the property, the owner has defaulted on mortgage payments and the lenders wish to sell with vacant possession, the landlord can also use this case.

Case 12 The landlord let accommodation which he or she intends to occupy on retirement. If the owner dies or if a mortgage lender wishes to repossess the property the same provisions apply as in Case 11.

Case 13 The property was let for a fixed term of not more than eight months and it had been occupied as a holiday letting within the previous 12 months (see page 54 for the definition of a holiday letting). The purpose of this case is to allow landlords who have holiday lettings in the summer to let on longer periods during the winter and then revert to holiday usage each year.

Case 14 The letting was for a fixed term of not more than 12 months and it had been occupied as a student letting during the preceding 12 months (see page 54 for the definition of a student letting).

Case 15 The accommodation had been let temporarily but is intended for letting to a minister of religion.

Cases 16, 17 & 18 These relate to various circumstances where properties are normally let to farm workers and have been let temporarily to ordinary tenants.

Case 19 The property was let on a protected shorthold tenancy and that tenancy has come to an end. For further details of protected shorthold tenancies see page 62.

Case 20 The landlord was a member of the armed forces at the time the tenancy started and intended to live in the house in the future. If the owner dies, a member of the family who was previously living with him or her and who wishes to live there again can also regain possession under this case. Anyone who inherits the property can regain possession under this case either if they want to live in it, or if they want to sell it with vacant possession. If there is a mortgage on the property, the lenders can use this case if they wish to sell with vacant possession. The case can also be used if the owner needs to sell with vacant possession to buy a home nearer to a place of work.

It is important to remember that the landlord **must** serve notice on the tenant at the beginning of the tenancy for any of these cases to apply. However, in cases 11 (returning owner occupier), 12 (retirement home), 19 (shorthold) and 20 (armed forces landlord) the court **may** grant possession even if the landlord has not fulfilled some of the necessary conditions if the court thinks it is just and equitable to do so. The court could therefore decide to waive the rule requiring the landlord to serve notice on the tenant at the start of the tenancy.

TENANTS WITH RESTRICTED CONTRACTS

Many tenants who are not regulated tenants and so do not have the full protection of the Rent Act have a more limited form of security. Tenants in this position have what is known in law as a *restricted contract*.[13] Only tenancies that began before 15 January 1989 can be restricted contracts. After that date, any agreement to change the rent will have the effect of ending the restricted contract and creating a tenancy with only basic protection (see page 72). However, a change in the rent registered by the Rent Tribunal will **not** bring an end to the restricted contract. The following people have restricted contracts:

- Tenants excluded from full protection because they have a *resident landlord* (see page 54). This is by far the largest group of tenants with restricted contracts.

- Tenants excluded from full protection because they share living accommodation with the landlord (see page 55).

- Tenants excluded from full protection because they make a payment for attendances which forms a *substantial* part of the rent (see page 53).

- Tenants excluded from full protection because they make a payment for board but this does **not** form a substantial part of the rent. (Where payment for board does form a substantial part of the rent, the tenant does not even have a restricted contract and has only the minimum protection available to tenants, see page 72.)

Restricted contracts: protection from evication

Landlords can only evict any tenant by following the proper legal procedures and gaining a possession order from the court. No tenant has to leave just because they have received a Notice to Quit from the landlord. If you have a restricted contract then the landlord does have the right to get you out eventually. But this can be delayed, sometimes by several months, and this delay can give you a chance to look around for another home.

The type of protection available to people with restricted contracts depends on whether the letting began before or after 28 November 1980.

Lettings made before 28 November 1980[14]

The protection available to tenants of these lettings depends on whether there is a *fixed term* or a *periodic* agreement. (See page 56 for definitions of these.)

- *Fixed term agreements:* Before the fixed term expires the landlord can only get a possession order if the tenant has broken one of the terms of the agreement and that agreement specifies that a possession order can be sought for that reason. After the fixed term has expired the landlord can go to court for a possession order and has an automatic right to one.

- *Periodic agreement:* Where there is a periodic agreement the landlord must first give a Notice to Quit in the proper form (see page 57). The tenant can, however, apply to the *Rent Tribunal* before the Notice to Quit runs out to have the notice deferred for up to six months. If the tribunal grants a deferment of the notice, the tenant can go back before the period runs out and ask for a further deferment, although it is not usual for more than one such extension to be granted. Once any extension has run out the landlord can go to court for a possession order and has an automatic right to one. The address and telephone number of your local Rent Tribunal can be found in the telephone directory.

Lettings made on or after 28 November 1980[15]

These tenants do not have the right to ask the Rent Tribunal to suspend a Notice to Quit. Instead, tenants (whether with fixed term or periodic agreements) can ask the court to suspend a possession order for up to **three months**. No extension beyond three months is possible.

PROTECTED SHORTHOLD TENANCIES

Shorthold tenancies were a new form of letting created by the Housing Act 1980.[16] The idea of a protected shorthold was that the landlord could let for a fixed period of time, during which the tenant is fully protected, but at the end of that time the landlord has a right to regain possession. The tenant also has a number of other rights.

For a tenancy to be a protected shorthold a number of conditions must be fulfilled:

- It must have started on or after 28 November 1980 and before 15 January 1989. From 15 January 1989 new shorthold tenancies will be *assured shortholds* (see page 71).
- It must be for a fixed period of between one and five years.
- At the start of the tenancy the landlord must give the tenant a notice in exactly the form laid down in law. The notice informs tenants of the fact that they are taking a shorthold and explains some (but not all) of their rights.
- The Rent Officer must have registered a *fair rent* for the accommodation (see page 91) or the Rent Officer must have issued a Certificate of Fair Rent (this is a formal statement by the Rent Officer of what a fair rent would be). The landlord must then apply, within 28 days of the start of the tenancy, for a fair rent to be registered. However, shortholds outside of London which began on or after 1 December 1981 and those in London which began on or after 4 May 1987 do not have to have a fair rent registered, although tenants are still entitled to apply to have a fair rent registered if they wish.
- An existing tenancy cannot under any circumstances be converted into a shorthold tenancy.

Protected shorthold tenancies: protection from eviction

During the fixed term, the shorthold is the same as any other fixed term tenancy: the landlord can only seek a possession order if you break the terms of the agreement and the agreement allows the landlord to seek possession in those circumstances. At the end of the fixed term if the landlord takes no action to get you out then you have the right to stay for at least an extra year. If the landlord wants to regain possession at the end of the fixed term then he or she must follow a fairly complex procedure. The landlord must give you a notice in writing during the last three months of the tenancy. The notice must give at least three months' warning of the landlord's intention to seek a possession order in the court. Then after that notice has expired the landlord must apply to the court not longer than three months from the date that the notice stated that he or she would be applying for a possession order.

If the agreed shorthold period expires and the landlord has *not* served a notice on the tenant that he or she intends to seek a possession order then the landlord has to wait another nine months before being able to serve such a notice. Similarly, if the landlord serves a notice of his or her intention to seek possession and then does not actually apply to the court in the three months allowed, then he or she has to wait another nine months before being able to serve such a notice.

Once the case comes to court the landlord will have to prove that the tenancy was a valid shorthold and that the proper notice procedure has been followed. However, the court can overlook a failure to follow two of the conditions if it considers it is just and equitable to do so. The two conditions it may overlook are:

- the requirement that a notice be given to the tenant in the prescribed form stating that the letting is a shorthold, **and**

- the requirement that a fair rent be registered or a certificate of fair rent issued at the correct time.

Remember that this section only applies to *protected shorthold* tenancies created before 15 January 1989. After that date different provisions apply to newly created shorthold tenancies (see page 71).

TIED HOUSING: A HOME WITH A JOB

This section applies to tenancies which began before 15 January 1989 **and** to those which began after that date. Some people take a job which includes accommodation, for example as a caretaker or a pub manager. This section deals with tied tenants in the private sector. Tenants in the public sector are dealt with on page 79 and agricultural workers in tied housing on page 64. People in tied housing may be either licensees (known as *service occupiers*) or tenants (known as *service tenants*) depending on their circumstances. The difference between the two is not defined in legislation but is based on judgments in court cases.

However, just because your employer and your landlord are the same person it does not mean that you automatically live in tied housing. You might, for example, be an ordinary private tenant who happens to be offered a job by your landlord. This would not by itself turn you into a tied tenant. The landlord has to prove that your home was taken *in consequence* of your job. Generally this means that you take up home and job together and that there is some connection between the two. If there is no such connection, you are an ordinary tenant or licensee.

Service occupiers: In order for your landlord to prove that you are merely a licensee, or service occupier, it must be shown that:

- either it is *necessary* for you to live in the accommodation in order to carry out your duties, **or**
- your contract of employment requires you to live there **and** that it is necessary for the *better performance* of your duties.

So, for example, it might be argued that it was necessary for a caretaker to live on the premises for security reasons. It is not enough simply to show that it is more convenient, for example because it is nearer to your work. If you are a service occupier who has exclusive possession of your home (see page 52 for what 'exclusive possession' means) then the landlord can only get you out by going to court for a possession order. You cannot just be told to leave.[17]

Service tenants: If the letting was *in consequence* of the job but is not necessary in either of the two ways listed above, then you are probably a *service tenant*. Service tenants have much the same rights as ordinary tenants and their security depends on whether they are assured tenants (see page 67), fully protected or have only restricted or basic security (see page 53). If the tenancy began before 15 January 1989 there is, however, an additional ground for eviction in the Rent Act, where the tenant has left the landlord's employment and the landlord now reasonably requires the property for a new employee (see page 58). If the tenancy began on or after 15 January 1989 then there is an additional ground for possession in the Housing Act 1988 (see page 71).

TIED HOUSING: AGRICULTURAL WORKERS

This section applies to tenancies which began before 15 January 1989. If your tenancy began on or after that date see page 72. Agricultural workers have special protection under the Rent (Agriculture) Act 1976 which added a complex layer to existing legislation. This section gives a brief outline of the protection available. Farm workers worried about losing their homes should get advice from their union or an advice centre.

The basis of the 1976 Act is that it gives security to those agricultural workers who are not protected by the Rent Act 1977. These occupiers are protected until suitable alternative accommodation is available and the Act puts obligations on local councils to help with alternative accommodation. To qualify for these benefits you must be in accommodation provided by your employer and have been working full time in agriculture for at least 91 weeks during the past two years.[18] These rights also apply to retired workers and can pass on to a surviving spouse or other family member who had been living in the cottage during the six months preceding the farm worker's death.[19] Farm workers employed and housed by government departments, the Crown or certain other public bodies are not covered by the Act, but administrative arrangements have been made to give them broadly the same benefits.

Agricultural workers: protected occupiers
In order to qualify for protection the occupier must have a tenancy or licence which meets certain conditions.[20] If you have a *licence* (see page 51) it must be one which allows exclusive occupation of the property and which if it had been a tenancy would have had Rent Act protection.

If you have a *tenancy*, again it must be of the kind which would have Rent Act protection. For the purposes of this Act, the following types of arrangement would also be included as being equivalent to lettings with Rent Act protection:

- lettings to occupiers who pay no or low rent;
- lettings of property on an agricultural holding;
- lettings where meals are provided in the course of employment and where any attendance provided is not substantial (see page 53 for what is meant by 'attendances' and 'substantial').

With these exceptions, the lettings must meet all the conditions which bring a tenancy within the Rent Act (see page 53 for a full description of these). Occupiers who meet these criteria have a protected occupancy.

Agricultural workers who have a resident landlord and those who live in hostels are not protected occupiers.

In order to gain possession from a protected occupier the employer must prove one of the following grounds:[21]

Case 1 Suitable alternative accommodation has been offered by a landlord other than the local authority.

Case 2 Alternative accommodation has been offered by the local authority.

Case 3	Rent arrears or breaking other conditions of the tenancy or licence agreement.
Case 4	Causing a nuisance or using the property for illegal purposes.
Case 5	Damaging the property.
Case 6	Damaging the furniture provided by the landlord.
Case 7	The tenant has given Notice to Quit.
Case 8	The tenant has illegally assigned, sublet, or parted with possession of the property.
Case 9	The landlord wants the property to live in, either personally or for his or her family, and it was purchased before 13 April 1976.
Case 10	Overcharging of subtenant.
Case 11	A returning owner occupier.
Case 12	The property is intended as a retirement home.
Case 13	Overcrowding.

The details of these grounds for possession are similar to the Rent Act grounds (see page 57).

Cases 1-10 are *discretionary,* meaning that the landlord must prove the case **and** the court must think it is *reasonable* to grant possession. Cases 11-13 are *mandatory*, meaning that if the case is proved the court must grant possession.

If the landlord wishes to gain possession, he or she can apply to the local council for suitable alternative accommodation for the occupier.[22] The landlord must show that the property is required in order that a new employee can be housed, that he or she cannot provide alternative accommodation and that the local council should provide alternative accommodation 'in the interests of efficient agriculture'. There is a procedure for the local council, the landlord or the occupier to refer the case to a local Agricultural Dwelling House Advisory Committee to advise on the issues involved. Where the council is satisfied of the applicant's case it must use its best endeavours to provide alternative accommodation.

Farm workers not protected by the Rent (Agriculture) Act 1976

Where an agricultural worker is not a protected occupier under the Act there are special provisions under the Protection from Eviction Act 1977 to give some limited rights.[23] The court has special powers to suspend a possession order and, if the order is made within six months of the end of the tenancy or licence the order **must** be suspended until the end of that six month period unless suitable alternative accommodation will be available, or there are other strong reasons for not suspending it.

ASSURED TENANCIES WHICH BEGAN BEFORE 15 JANUARY 1989

This was a new type of tenancy introduced by the Housing Act 1980.[24] At present there are only a handful of them. All assured tenancies will, after 15 January 1989, be subject to the provisions of the Housing Act 1988 (see below).

TENANCIES WHICH BEGAN ON OR AFTER 15 JANUARY 1989

The Housing Act 1988 introduces major changes to the law on renting from private landlords and housing associations. The Act introduces two new types of lettings: assured and assured shorthold tenancies. Most tenancies which began before 15 January 1989 will not be affected and will keep the same legal protection. After that date there will be no new protected tenancies (or secure housing association tenancies) unless:[25]

- the tenancy was agreed before that date; **or**
- the tenant was previously the fully protected tenant (see pages 50-60) (or secure housing association tenant (see pages 79-85)) of the same landlord; **or**
- the new tenancy is being granted as suitable alternative accommodation as part of a possession order and the court has directed that a protected tenancy (or secure housing association tenancy) is granted.

The next four sections on pages 67-72 give details of the new types of tenancy.

ASSURED TENANCIES: TENANCIES EXCLUDED FROM PROTECTION

After 15 January 1989 lettings by private landlords and housing associations will be assured tenancies unless they are one of the following types of tenancy:[26]

- Tenancies that were entered into or agreed before 15 January 1989.
- *Homes where the rateable value is very high:* If the rateable value is above £1500 in Greater London or above £750 elsewhere. There are very few properties with rateable values above these limits.
- *Tenancies where the rent is very low:* Where no rent is paid or the rent is less than two thirds of the rateable value. Payments for rates, services, maintenance and insurance are not included in calculating the rent. Again

this affects a very small number of tenancies.

- *Business tenancies* to which Part II of the Landlord and Tenant Act 1954 applies.
- *Licensed premises:* Tenancies of dwellings licensed for the sale of alcohol on the premises.
- *Agricultural land:* Tenancies let with over two acres of agricultural land and holdings occupied by the person responsible for farming the land.
- *Lettings to students by educational institutions:* The institutions have to be approved by the Department of the Environment.
- *Holiday lettings:* See page 54 for the definition of a holiday letting.
- *Resident landlords:* To qualify as resident the landlord must have lived in the same building as the tenant, continuously since the start of the tenancy. The landlord does not count as resident, however, if the building is a purpose built block of flats.
- *Crown Tenancies:* The landlord is the Crown or a government department.
- *Public sector tenancies:* Tenants of local councils, new towns, housing co-operatives, housing action trusts and other public housing bodies. However, housing association tenancies can be assured tenancies (see page 79).
- Protected tenancies (see pages 50-66), existing housing association tenancies (see pages 79-85), and tenancies protected by the Rent (Agriculture) Act 1976 (see pages 64-65), as long as these tenancies started before 15 January 1989.

ASSURED TENANTS: PROTECTION FROM EVICTION

Assured tenants can only be evicted by a court order. They do not have to leave just because the landlord tells them to or because the tenancy agreement has run out. Anyone whose landlord asks them to leave should get advice immediately.

If the original tenancy was for a *fixed term* only, for example six months or a year, and when that time runs out the landlord does not offer you a new tenancy of the same premises, then the assured tenancy automatically becomes a *periodic tenancy* which means that it continues indefinitely and the landlord can only evict you by going to court and proving one of the grounds for eviction set out below.[27]

Notice of proceedings for possession

Where the landlord wants to seek a possession order against an assured tenant, he or she must first give the tenant a notice of proceedings for possession in the proper legal form. The notice must specify which of the Grounds for Possession (set out in the next section) the landlord is seeking to prove. The landlord must give at least two months notice if Grounds 1, 2, 5, 6, 7, 9 or 16 are specified in the written notice or at least two weeks notice if any of the other grounds are specified.

Normally, the landlord cannot go to court unless a proper notice of seeking possession has been served on the tenant. However, the court can decide to waive this rule, if it considers it just and equitable to do so, in any case except one where the landlord is seeking possession on Ground 8 below.[28]

Grounds for possession

If the tenancy is for a fixed term and it has not yet expired, the landlord can only go to court for a possession order on Grounds 2, 8, or 10-15 below and the tenancy agreement states that the tenancy can be ended for that reason.[29]

If the tenancy is for an indefinite period (a periodic tenancy) the landlord can try to persuade the court that he or she should get a possession order on any of the grounds listed below.[30]

For the first set of Grounds 1-8, the court must order possession if the ground is proved.

Grounds 1-5 require that the landlord served notice on the tenant before the tenancy began that possession might be sought on these grounds, although in the case of Grounds 2 and 3 the court can waive this requirement if it considers it just and equitable to do so.

Ground 1 Before the start of the tenancy the landlord had at some time occupied the accommodation as his or her only or principal home, or the property is required as the only or principal home for the landlord and his or her spouse and the landlord did not buy the property with the tenants already living there.

Ground 2 A mortgage lender requires vacant possession of the property to sell it.

Ground 3 The property was let for a fixed term of not more than eight months.

and it had been occupied as a holiday letting within the previous 12 months (see page 54 for the definition of a holiday letting).

Ground 4 The tenancy was for a fixed term of not more than 12 months and it had been occupied as a student letting within the preceding 12 months.

Ground 5 The accommodation has been let temporarily but is now required for letting to a minister of religion.

Ground 6 The landlord intends to demolish, reconstruct or carry out substantial work on the property and five conditions are fulfilled. First, that the tenant is not willing to allow the landlord to gain access to do the works or it would be impracticable to gain the necessary access. Second, that the tenant is not willing to move into only part of the accommodation to allow the work to be carried out or it would be impractical for the tenant to do so. Third, that the landlord cannot reasonably carry out the work without gaining possession of the property. Fourth, that the landlord did not buy the property with the tenants already living there. Fifth, that the assured tenancy did not come into being as a result of the present tenant gaining the right to succeed to a previous fully protected tenant who had died.

Ground 7 The tenant inherited the tenancy under the will or intestacy of the previous tenant and the landlord has begun possession proceedings not later than twelve months after the death of the former tenant or from the date at which the court decides the landlord became aware of the death.

Ground 8 There are at least three months rent arrears both when the notice of proceedings for possession is served on the tenant and at the date of the court hearing.

For the second set of Grounds for Possession 9-16, the court may grant a possession order but only if the landlord can prove the case and the court thinks that it is reasonable to grant an order. The court also has the power to suspend any possession order either for a fixed period, or indefinitely subject to certain conditions — for example the court might make an order for possession under Ground 10 because of rent arrears but suspend the order to give the tenant an opportunity to pay off the arrears. Then, as long as the tenant pays off the agreed amounts, the order will not take effect.

Ground 9 Suitable alternative accommodation is available for the tenant. In deciding whether the alternative accommodation is suitable the court must take account of the degree of protection from eviction it offers, the rent charged, the type and size of property offered and its distance from your work. This does not mean, however, that the alternative on offer necessarily has to be of the same standard as your present home.

Ground 10 There are rent arrears both when the notice of proceedings for possession is served on the tenant and when the possession proceedings begin.

Ground 11 The tenant has persistently delayed paying the rent, whether or not there are outstanding arrears when the possession proceedings are begun.

Ground 12 The tenant has broken one of the terms of the tenancy agreement.

Ground 13 The tenant or someone else living in their home has damaged or neglected the property.

Ground 14 The tenant or someone else living in their home has caused a nuisance or annoyance to neighbours or has been convicted of using the property for illegal or immoral purposes.

Ground 15 The tenant or someone else living in their home has damaged furniture provided by the landlord.

Ground 16 The property was let in consequence of the tenant's employment by the landlord or a previous landlord of the property and the tenant is no longer in that employment.

ASSURED SHORTHOLD TENANCIES

Assured shorthold tenancies are a new type of tenancy which begin on or after 15 January 1989. If you have a shorthold tenancy which began before that date see pages 62-63.

Assured shorthold tenancies are exactly the same as other assured tenancies (see pages 67-71), except that the landlord is entitled to get a court order to evict the shorthold tenant once the agreed period of the tenancy has come to an end without having to prove any other grounds for the order. However, the landlord must follow the proper legal procedures to do this.[31]

First, the tenancy must be for a period of at least six months. Second, before the tenancy begins the landlord must serve a notice on the tenant in exactly the form laid down in law. The notice informs tenants of the fact that the tenancy is a shorthold. Third, the landlord must give the tenant at least two months' notice in the correct legal form and at the right time that he or she requires possession of the property. Fourth, the landlord must get a court order.

TENANTS WITH RESIDENT LANDLORDS

This section applies only to tenancies which began on or after 15 January 1989. If your tenancy began before that date see pages 60-62. After that date, the protection from eviction of tenants of resident landlords will depend on whether or not they share living accommodation with the owner or his or her family in their only or principal home.[32] If you do share such living accommodation then the landlord can evict you without even needing to get a court order. If your landlord is resident in the building (see page 54 for what is meant by resident) but you do not share any such living accommodation with the landlord or his or her family then you will still have basic protection. See below for what this means.

ASSURED AGRICULTURAL OCCUPANCIES

Agricultural workers who live in tied housing and whose occupancy began on or after 15 January 1989 will have special protection under the Housing Act 1988.[33] The type of protection and those covered by it will be broadly the same as the provisions of the Rent (Agriculture) Act 1976. For details see the section on pages 64-66, except that references to the Rent Act will now be to the Housing Act 1988 and the list of grounds for possession on pages 65-66 will now be replaced by Grounds 1-15 listed on pages 68-69. Ground 16 does not apply to assured agricultural occupiers.

ALL TENANTS

TENANTS WITH ONLY BASIC PROTECTION

Tenants who have only basic protection are those who are excluded from both full and restricted protection. This will normally be because:

- You are provided with substantial board, for example meals (see page 53) and your tenancy began before 15 January 1989.
- You have a holiday letting (see page 54) which began before 15 January 1989.
- You had a restricted contract which ended when the rent was increased (see page 60) or a tenancy with a resident landlord which began on or after 15 January 1989 and you do not share any rooms with the landlord.

In most cases the landlord still has to get a possession order from the court in order to evict you and any other attempt at eviction is illegal.[16] If there is a fixed term agreement the landlord cannot evict you before the agreement has expired unless you break the agreement. If there is no fixed term agreement the landlord must give a Notice to Quit in the proper form (see page 57) before going to court.[34] However, some tenants and licensees are excluded from this protection (see page 143).

SHARERS

People who share a rented home often regard themselves as having equal legal rights in it. But, in fact, their legal positions may be quite different and can be very complicated. They could be tenants, subtenants, licensees or a combination of these.

Joint tenants

The simplest position is where the group of sharers all took the tenancy together and where all their names are on the tenancy agreement or rent book. They hold as a group and individually all the rights and responsibilities of individual tenants. So, for example, they are jointly and individually responsible for keeping to the tenancy agreement and paying the rent. If one tenant fails to pay their share of the rent the others will be equally responsible for any arrears. They have the same protection from eviction as individual tenants in the same circumstances.

However, complications can arise if one of the tenants leaves and is replaced by a different person. The best approach is to agree the replacement with the landlord. If this is not done the new sharer may be only a subtenant or even a licensee of the remaining tenants.

Subtenants

If a tenant of a property sublets all or part of it to someone else, that person is known as a *subtenant.* The legal position can become very complicated because there are now three sets of relationships involved: landlord and tenant; tenant and subtenant; and landlord and subtenant. This section gives a broad outline of the legal position but anyone in doubt about their status should get legal advice.

If the tenancy began before 15 January 1989 a tenant is allowed to sublet a *part* of the property if this is not forbidden in the tenancy agreement. If the tenancy is an assured tenancy that began on or after 15 January 1989 then you are not allowed to sublet without the landlord's agreement. In practice most agreements do prohibit subletting and any subtenancies created despite the prohibition are known as illegal subtenancies. Even if subletting is prohibited, however, it may be possible to have people staying simply as lodgers or licensees, unless this is also forbidden in the agreement (it may, for example, forbid taking in 'paying guests'). A regulated tenant can be evicted if he or she sublets *all* of the property without the landlord's consent.[35]

When subletting is not forbidden

If subletting is not forbidden then you might consider doing this. But you will need to make sure that the subletting does not create overcrowding (see page 129) and that the subtenant does not damage the landlord's property or furniture or cause a nuisance to neighbours. In addition, if you are a regulated tenant you must not charge more than is allowed under the Rent Act (see page 91). If any of these things happen then these could be grounds for the landlord to seek a possession order against you.

If you are not a regulated tenant then subletting without full knowledge and consent of the landlord would be most inadvisable since your landlord can evict you.

When subletting is forbidden

If subletting is prohibited but you do it anyway, then the landlord will have a case for seeking a possession order. However, if you can show that the landlord knew about the subtenant and took no action, it may be possible to argue that tacit consent had been given. If you change your mind and want to evict the subtenant you cannot do so on the grounds that the original subletting was illegal (although you may have other grounds for a possession order).

The subtenant's protection from eviction

As long as the tenant continues to hold the tenancy, then he or she is the landlord of the subtenant. The security of the subtenant is decided in the same way as for any other tenant. In most instances the tenant is a resident landlord and the subtenant will usually have restricted or perhaps only basic protection depending on their circumstances (see page 60).

Even if subletting was forbidden, the landlord cannot evict the subtenant without evicting the tenant at the same time. If the tenant is evicted or gives up the tenancy, then the subtenant's position depends first on whether or not subletting was forbidden. If subletting was forbidden then, once the tenant has gone, the landlord can normally evict the subtenant. If subletting was *not* forbidden then the subtenant's security depends on the degree of protection enjoyed by the tenant and by the subtenant in relation to the tenant. In the unlikely event that the subtenant was fully protected in relation to a protected tenant then, if the tenant leaves, the subtenant becomes the direct, fully protected tenant of the landlord.[36] If either the subtenant or the tenant were *not* fully protected then the landlord can normally evict the subtenant once the tenant has left. The position of assured tenants is similar. If an assured tenant's immediate landlord is the tenant of another landlord and the immediate landlord's tenancy comes to an end, the subtenant becomes the assured tenant of the head landlord.[37]

Sharers who are licensees

It is common in flat shares for one person to be named on the tenancy agreement and for this person to take responsibility for dealings with the landlord. There is usually no written agreement between this person and the other sharers. In these circumstances it is quite likely that they are not joint tenants. The other sharers may be subtenants or merely licensees of the tenant who deals with the landlord. It is often difficult to establish the legal status of flat sharers but the informality of many flat sharing arrangements, where people split household bills and even food costs (rather than having the formal arrangement typical of landlords and tenants) suggests that the sharers may simply be the licensees of the tenant named on the agreement with the landlord. However, if it can be demonstrated that the sharers live as separate households, this would tend to suggest subtenancies. The dividing line between a tenancy and a licence is not clear (see page 51) but sharers are **not** necessarily all licensees just because none of them has exclusive occupation of one part of the flat. If they rented the flat from the landlord **as a group** with only one tenancy agreement for all of them then they will probably be joint tenants. As can be seen, these cases are often very complex and anyone in this position should seek good legal advice.

TENANTS OF LANDLORDS WITH MORTAGES

Many tenants have landlords who have a mortgage on the property which was taken out before the tenancy began. Most mortgage agreements prohibit letting and these tenants are in a similar position to illegal subtenants. In relation to their landlord they will have the same degree of protection as any other tenant, but in relation to the lender the tenant has no protection. So if the lender repossesses the property the tenant can be evicted.

If, however, the mortgage was taken out **after** you became a tenant of the property then your security will not be affected. If the lender repossesses the property from the landlord they also take over his or her position in relation to the tenant and your degree of legal protection remains the same.

LICENSEES: PROTECTION FROM EVICTION

The difference between a licensee and a tenant is explained on page 51. A licensee may be:

- a service occupier (see page 63);
- a licensee with restricted protection;
- a licensee without restricted protection.

Licensees with restricted protection

A few licensees have *restricted protection.*[38] In order to qualify for this protection **all** the following must apply:

- the licence agreement began before 15 January 1989 **and** there has been no agreed change in the rent payable since that date, **and**

- you have exclusive possession of at least part of the property, **and**

- the property is used as your home, **and**

- there is some payment for furniture or services. Services cover more than just attendance (see page 54) and include heating, lighting, hot water etc. But if you are provided with substantial board or it is a holiday arrangement then you do not have a restricted contract.

A landlord who wants to evict a licensee with restricted protection must first bring the licence to an end by giving the proper notice. This must be of the length of time specified in the agreement, or 'reasonable notice', whichever is the longer. It does not have to be in writing unless this is specified in the licence agreement. What the court would consider reasonable notice depends on individual circumstances, particularly how long the licensee has lived there. Someone who has lived in their home for a considerable time could perhaps expect to receive four weeks' notice. Licensees with restricted protection have the same rights as restricted tenants to delay eviction. These rights are described on page 60.

All licensees

Many licensees whether or not they have restricted protection, do come within the Protection from Eviction Act 1977, which means that the landlord must give them proper notice and get a court order before evicting them. For further details see page 143. If your licence agreement is not for a fixed period and it is not one of those excluded from the Protection from Eviction Act (see page 144), then the landlord *must* give you written notice to quit of at least four weeks in the proper legal form.

GOING TO COURT

When the landlord wants to take you to court to evict you, the next step after the Notice to Quit (if one is required, see page 143), or notice of possession proceedings (see page 69) or a notice ending a licence, is that you will receive a summons from the court. In most cases you will also receive a form which allows you either to admit the landlord's case or to state your defence. If you wish to, you can also make a claim against the landlord (known as a *counterclaim*), for example for damages for any repairs which have not been done. This form should be returned to the court within 14 days. If you have not yet got legal advice do so immediately and get help in filling in the form before returning it. If you fail to return the form within the 14 days, return it as soon as possible after that with an explanation for the delay. If solicitors are acting for you they will probably not use the form sent by the court but will lodge a defence and counterclaim on their own stationery. If you have sent in a defence, then the first court hearing will normally be a *pre-trial review* at which the judge will set down a timetable for the preparations for the trial. If you have good reasons for not having had a chance to submit a defence you can ask for a chance to do this and for the case to be heard at a later date. However, you cannot use this simply as a delaying tactic and you may also find that you have to pay the landlord's legal costs for that day, regardless of the outcome of the case. These costs may be considerable.

When the case comes to court, you can speak for yourself, but courts can be very intimidating and your chances will be better if you can get a solicitor or barrister to represent you. However close it is to the court hearing you may still be able to win the case. If the case has already been to court and you think a mistaken judgment has been given you may be able to appeal against it. Get advice as soon as possible. You may qualify for legal aid to help with any costs (see page 166).

If the judge grants a possession order, you or your representative can ask for it to be suspended. If it is suspended be sure that you understand fully any conditions which the judge makes; for example, how much of any arrears you must pay off each week. Do not agree to pay off more than you can afford. If you find you cannot meet the conditions, it is possible to go back to the court to ask for them to be changed, although the judge will not necessarily agree to this. If you have met all the conditions (for example paying off all the arrears) you can go back to court to get the order discharged. It is a good idea to do this as it prevents the landlord using it against you again at a future date.

The judge will usually postpone the date on which you must give possession of the property for a short period. In most cases this period is at the judge's discretion and 28 days is fairly commonly allowed. However, in certain cases (notably Rent Act cases 11-20 on page 59 where the court is obliged to grant an order if the case is proved), the court can normally only allow 14 days, with a maximum of six weeks in cases of exceptional hardship.[39] The court cannot postpone the eviction date if the order is granted against an assured shorthold tenant or an assured tenant on one of grounds 1-8 on page 69.[40]

In addition to these normal procedures, there are some special procedures for speedier evictions in certain very limited circumstances. If the landlord is seeking possession on one of the Rent Act cases 11-20 (see page 59) then he or she is entitled to use a speedier procedure. On cases 11, 12 and 20 only seven days' notice of the hearing need be given; on cases 13-19, 14 days' notice is required.[41] However, if the landlord uses this special procedure, the court is not allowed to waive the requirement that notice should have been served on the tenant at the start of the tenancy that these grounds for eviction might be used (see page 60 for details of this rule).

An even quicker procedure is available for use against trespassers who are either squatters or licensees whose licence has been ended by the landlord. The landlord can arrange for a court hearing without even knowing the names of the occupiers. Normally not less than five days' notice of the hearing is given, but the court can allow an even shorter period. Normally the possession order is not postponed, but where the occupiers were originally licensees the court can postpone the order.[42]

THE EVICTION

When the date for possession has arrived the next step is that the landlord can apply to the court for a warrant of possession which enables the bailiffs, who are court officers, to carry out the eviction. The bailiffs will normally give a few days' notice of the eviction, although they do not have to do so.

It is important to note that if the possession order is suspended on certain conditions (for example, payment of arrears) and you break those conditions, the landlord does not normally have to go back to the judge but can go straight to the bailiffs for eviction. If, however, this happens and you believe you have not broken any of the conditions of the suspended order then you can go to court to get the eviction stopped. You will need immediate legal advice to do this as you may only have a few days.

Illegal evictions and harassment

If the landlord tries to get you out by any other means than the legal steps defined in this section then he or she is acting illegally. See page 143 for more details of protection from harassment and illegal eviction.

THE KEY QUESTIONS FOR PRIVATE TENANTS

The law relating to protection from eviction for private tenants is complicated. The key questions to answer, with the help of this section, are:

○ **Are you a licensee or a tenant** (page 51)?

○ If you are a **tenant** are you:
A regulated tenant (page 53)
A restricted contract tenant (page 60)
A protected shorthold tenant (page 62)
A service tenant (page 63)
An assured tenant (page 67)
An assured shorthold tenant (page 71)
A tenant with only basic protection (page 72)
A sub tenant (page 73)
A joint tenant (page 73)
A tenant of a mortgagor (page 75)?

○ If you are a **licensee,** are you:
A service occupier (page 63)
A licensee with restricted protection (page 60)?

○ If you are an **agricultural worker** do you qualify for protection under the Rent (Agriculture) Act 1976 or the Housing Act 1988 (pages 64 & 72)?

If you are in any doubt about your position see Chapter 7, *Getting advice and legal representation.*

Council tenants, housing association tenants and tenants of other public landlords

Since 1980, the great majority of council, housing association and other tenants of public sector landlords have had protection from eviction. Their landlords can only evict if they can prove to a court that one of a very limited number of *grounds for possession* exists. So, normally tenants who pay their rent and do not break the tenancy agreement are completely secure in their homes.

HOUSING ASSOCIATION TENANTS

If your tenancy began before 15 January 1989 you should read the following sections for secure tenants. If your tenancy began on or after 15 January 1989 you will be covered by the provisions of the Housing Act 1988 on assured tenancies (see pages 67-72).

SECURE TENANTS

The vast majority of public sector tenants are secure and (unlike in the private sector) licensees have the same legal protection as tenants. The only exceptions to this are:

- where they first entered their home as squatters and were then given a temporary licence for that or another property by the landlord. These ex-squatter licensees do not have the same protection as tenants.
- Residents in hostels provided by councils and housing associations do not have protection from eviction.[43]

Tenants of all of the following landlords count as secure tenants:[44]

- a local authority;
- the Housing Corporation;
- a housing trust which is registered as a charity; or
- a housing association registered with the Housing Corporation or with an application for registration pending (but not co-ownership associations) if the tenancy began before 15 January 1989. If your tenancy began after that date see pages 67-72;
- a new town development corporation;
- the Commission for the New Towns;
- the Development Board for Rural Wales;
- a housing co-operative where the properties are owned by the local council (tenants of co-operatives where the properties are owned by the co-op itself are not secure tenants);
- an urban development corporation.

Tenants of the Crown are not secure tenants, but many do have some legal protection. Get advice if you are a tenant of the crown or a government department.

In order to be secure the tenant must be a person (not a company) and the property must be their only or main home.[45]

There is a long list of types of public tenancy which are excluded from security, but the actual numbers of tenants involved are very small.[46] The exclusions are:

- Long leases of over 21 years.

- Tied accommodation where your contract of employment requires you to occupy your home for the better performance of your duties and you are employed by the landlord or by a local authority, a new town development corporation, the Commission for the New Towns, the Development Board for Rural Wales, or an urban development corporation.

- You are a member of the police force and your home is provided rent free.

- You work for the fire brigade, your contract of employment requires you to live close to a fire station and your home was let to you so that you could do so.

- Tied accommodation where you are employed by your landlord **and** your tenancy agreement states that the tenancy will end at the same time as your employment ends **and** the accommodation is held by the landlord for educational or social services purposes **and** the accommodation is part of or within the grounds of an educational or social services building. This covers accommodation for people such as school caretakers and residential social workers.

- Homes on land acquired for redevelopment and which are being used for temporary housing. This covers, for example, short life housing (see page 45).

- A tenancy given to you because you have applied for housing as a homeless person (see page 16) and you have the tenancy on a temporary basis for less than a year because:
  — the council is making enquiries about whether you qualify for permanent housing as a homeless person, **or**
  — the council has no long-term responsibility because you are intentionally homeless, **or**
  — the council is considering whether you have a local connection with another area.

- Temporary accommodation given to you for less than a year so that you could move to take up a job in that area or a neighbouring area. The landlord must notify you at the beginning of the tenancy that it is on this basis.

- The landlord has leased the property from a private landlord and then sublet to you on a temporary basis.

- Temporary accommodation provided to you while work is carried out on your usual home and you are **not** a secure tenant in your usual home.

- Student lettings where you are attending a course which has been designated for this purpose by the government. The landlord must notify you at the beginning of the tenancy that it is on this basis.

- Business tenancies, agricultural holdings and licensed premises.

- Almshouses.

- Tenancies granted before 8 May 1980 where the landlord is a charity and told you before the start of the tenancy that they would need to evict you to carry out work on the building.

Protection from eviction for secure tenants

The great majority of public sector tenants are secure and can only be evicted on very limited grounds. If the landlord believes that one of these grounds exists then the first thing they must do is give you a notice, usually known as a *notice of intended proceedings* or *a notice of seeking possession.*[47] This notice must be in the correct form laid down by the Department of the Environment[48] and must tell you the grounds on which the landlord is seeking to evict you. It should normally give a date, at least four weeks ahead, after which the case may be taken to court. This notice only remains in force for one year after that date. It then lapses and if the landlord wants to try again to evict you, they will have to give you a new notice.

Once the date given on the notice has passed, the next step is for the landlord to go to court to prove that one of the *grounds for possession* set out below applies to you.[49] The first six grounds are *discretionary* for the court, which means that the court may grant a possession order but only if the landlord can prove the case and the court thinks that it is reasonable to grant an order. The court also has the power to suspend any possession order, either for a fixed period, or indefinitely subject to certain conditions. For example, the court might make an order for possession because of rent arrears but suspend the order to give you an opportunity to pay off the arrears. Then, as long as you pay off the agreed amount, the order will not take effect. Public sector landlords are generally socially responsible and do not wish to evict tenants. So if, for example, they do get a possession order for rent arrears, they may themselves choose not to go ahead with the eviction straight away, so as to give you a chance to pay off the arrears.

The discretionary grounds for possession are:

Ground 1 You have rent arrears or have broken any obligation in the tenancy agreement.

Ground 2 You or anyone living with you cause nuisance to neighbours or are convicted of using the property for immoral or illegal purposes.

Ground 3 You, or anyone living with you, damage the property or part of the building shared with other tenants.

Ground 4 You, or anyone living with you, damage furniture provided by the landlord.

Ground 5 You got the tenancy by knowingly or recklessly making false statements to the council.

Ground 6 You have exchanged your home with another tenant and either paid money to, or received money from, the other tenant as a condition of making the exchange.

Ground 7 Your home goes with your job, it is part of larger premises which are not used mainly for housing (for example, a school) and someone living in the tenancy is guilty of misconduct which would make it not right for him or her to continue to live there.

Ground 8 You have been moved to another property while building work is carried out in your home and you then refuse to leave the temporary accommodation to return to your original home.

For the next three grounds for possession, the court must grant a possession order if the landlord can prove the case, but the landlord must also prove that *suitable alternative accommodation* is available for you (see below for what counts as suitable alternative accommodation). These grounds are:

Ground 9 You break the law by overcrowding your home (see page 129 for what counts as illegal overcrowding).

Ground 10 The landlord wants to demolish or do work on the building and cannot do so while it is occupied.

Ground 10A Your home is in an area for which there is a redevelopment scheme and the landlord plans, as part of the scheme, to sell the property. If the landlord wants to use this ground for possession, they must give you details of their plans, allow you at least 28 days to comment on them and then take your views into account. The redevelopment scheme must be approved by the Secretary of State for the Environment or, where the landlord is a registered housing association, by the Housing Corporation. If you are evicted on this ground you will be eligible for a home loss payment (see page 21) as well as being entitled to suitable alternative accommodation.

Ground 11 The landlord is a charity and your occupation of the property conflicts with the objects of the charity. For example, the charity's objectives may be to help people with disabilities and there may now be no one with a disability living in the accommodation.

For the next five grounds for possession the court may grant a possession order only if it considers both that it is *reasonable* to do so **and** that *suitable alternative accommodation* is available. These grounds for possession are:

Ground 12 Your home was let to you in consequence of your employment, it is part of premises not mainly used for housing, you no longer work in that job and the landlord needs the property for another employee.

Ground 13 The property has been specially designed for a person with a physical disability, there is no one with a disability living there and the landlord needs it for such a tenant.

Ground 14 Your landlord is a housing association or housing trust which lets only to special groups of people who have difficulty in getting housing, there is no longer such a person living there or you have received an offer of a secure tenancy from the local council, and the landlord needs the accommodation for a person from the special groups for whom it caters. The special groups could include people with, for example, particular handicaps, but this ground does not cover associations which let to people because of their low income and could not be used to evict someone because they were no longer on a low income.

Ground 15 The property is one of a group let to people with particular needs and is near a special facility (for example, an old people's club); there is no longer such a person living there and the council needs the property for someone with those special needs.

Ground 16 The previous tenant has died, a member of the family has taken over the tenancy and the home is larger than he or she needs. The landlord can only seek possession on this ground between six and 12 months after the tenant's death and it cannot be used against the widow or widower of the previous tenant or against someone who was a joint tenant with the person who has died. In deciding whether it is reasonable to grant a possession order on this ground the court has to take into account the age of the remaining tenant, how long he or she has lived there and any financial or other support given by him or her to the previous tenant.

Where the landlord has to prove that *suitable alternative accommodation* is available,[50] this has to be an offer of another home which is suitable for you and your family, taking account of where you work, where your children go to school and whether it is essential that you live close to a member of your family. Whether the offer is suitable can depend on the types of home being let to other people in the area (for example, if there are a larger number of flats in the area you might only be offered a flat rather than a house). But it is the court that decides whether or not the alternative accommodation is suitable and you can dispute the landlord's offer in court if you think it is not.

There are many ways in which you might be able to defend yourself in court. If the landlord has not served a proper Notice of Seeking Possession they are not entitled to proceed with the case. The landlord must produce evidence on why they believe they are entitled to evict you. You can challenge that evidence. In the cases where they must also prove that it is *reasonable* to evict you, you can argue in court that it is not reasonable. For example, if they have not given you a chance to pay off rent arrears, or to change the behaviour they are complaining of, you could argue it is not reasonable to evict you. If the landlord does not give you enough details of the reasons why they think they should have a possession order then again you can dispute the case in court.

Even if the court decides to grant a possession order, the judge often decides to suspend it. If, for example, a tenant gets into rent arrears, the court may suspend the order to give the tenant a chance to pay off the arrears. In these circumstances you need to agree with the landlord and the court a regular amount that will be paid off the arrears. This should be an amount you can afford and the court should not try to make you pay off an amount which would cause you any exceptional hardship. As long as you keep to this agreement you should not be in danger of eviction.

There have been many cases of tenants successfully defending themselves. Any tenant who receives a Notice of Seeking Possession should get advice immediately, so as to give as much time as possible to work out a defence. Even if a possession order has been granted against you, get advice if you have not already done so. It may be possible to appeal against the order, or at least delay the eviction. See page 76 for more details on going to court.

Home owners

Home owners have a high degree of security and there are only very limited circumstances in which they might lose their homes.

MORTGAGE ARREARS

If you do not keep up your mortgage payments the lender will eventually be able to evict you and sell the property to get their money back. If you have difficulties keeping up the payments see page 100. Even if you are taken to court you can still try to persuade the judge to grant a suspended possession order to give you a chance to pay off the arrears. If you are in danger of losing your home in this way get advice immediately. The number of home owners who have lost their homes because of mortgage arrears has been growing and it is important not to over-commit yourself by taking on a mortgage which you can only just afford and which you could not afford if there was a drop in your income.

ACTION BY THE LOCAL COUNCIL

In rare circumstances the council may make a compulsory purchase order on an owner-occupied property. It may do this in order to demolish the property, particularly if it is in a slum clearance area. There will normally have to be an enquiry held into any proposal for compulsory purchase and owners who wish to oppose the plans can get their legal costs paid. Owners (and tenants) who lose their homes in this way have a right to rehousing by the council and to compensation (see page 21). In addition to this compensation, home owners can claim an *owner occupier's supplement* if they have been living in the property (normally for at least two years) to make up the compensation to the owner to the full market value of the house.[51]

LONG LEASEHOLDERS: PROTECTION FROM EVICTION

Almost all flats and some houses are owned on long leases rather than outright. Many of these leases will last long beyond the lifetime of the owners and so there is no worry about what happens when they run out. But some leases, particularly on older houses, are running out. When this happens the leaseholder still has a right to stay indefinitely. However, the landlord can serve a notice that you should become a *statutory tenant.*[52] You would then stay on paying rent. There is one additional ground for possession under this procedure. If the landlord is a local authority or other public body they can seek possession if they propose to demolish or reconstruct all or most of the property. However this ground is rarely used.[53] If you live in a *house* (but not a flat) you also have rights under the Leasehold Reform Act 1967. This Act gives you the right to buy the freehold of the house from the landlord, usually for a very low sum, or to extend the lease for 50 years beyond the date it ended. You must claim this right before the lease expires and you must have been living there as your only or main home for at least three years or for three out of the last 10 years.

The price of buying the freehold can be fixed by agreement or, if you cannot agree with the landlord, by the Leasehold Valuation Tribunal. Prices of freeholds can be very low and if you are thinking of buying one you should get a qualified surveyor to advise you.

Mobile homes

If you own a mobile home, rent a pitch for it on a site and live there as your main home, you are protected by the Mobile Homes Act 1983. (If you *rent* the home you will be covered by the laws for tenants.) The Act does not cover you if you only use the home for holidays.[54]

PROTECTION FROM EVICTION

The Mobile Homes Act 1983 gives owners the right to keep their homes on the site they occupy indefinitely.[55] There can only be a fixed time limit on the agreement if the site owner's planning permission or right to use the land is itself limited to a fixed period. If this time limit is later extended, then so is your right to stay there. The resident can bring the agreement to an end by giving at least four weeks' notice in writing. The site owner can only bring the agreement to an end by applying to the County Court or to an arbitrator (see the section on *Settling disputes,* page 89). There are only three grounds on which the site owner can seek to end an agreement:

- You are not living in the mobile home as your main residence.
- The mobile home is having a detrimental effect on the site because of its age and condition or is likely to have this effect within the next five years. The site owner can only try to use this ground for ending the agreement once in any five year period, starting from the date the agreement began.
- You have broken one of the terms of the agreement and the court or arbitrator thinks it is reasonable to end the agreement. The site owner

must first tell you that you have broken the agreement and give you reasonable time to put things right.

If the site owner can prove to the court or arbitrator that the agreement should be brought to an end for one of these reasons the site owner can then get an eviction order from the court. Arbitrators cannot make eviction orders. The site owner can normally go to court to ask to end the agreement and for an eviction order at the same time.

If the site is privately owned the court can suspend an eviction order for up to one year, but cannot suspend it if the site is owned by the local council. It is a criminal offence for the site owner to evict you without a court order; to harass or threaten you; or to cut off services such as gas, electricity or water so as to get you to leave.[56] If you have any of these problems, get advice.

The site owner can make you move to another part of the site **only** if:[57]

- your agreement says that this can be done, **and**
- the new pitch is broadly comparable to the old one, **and**
- the site owner pays all the costs.

THE RIGHT TO A WRITTEN AGREEMENT AND TO A STATEMENT OF RIGHTS

The site owner must give you a written statement of your legal rights and the terms of your agreement.[58] This agreement cannot change the rights set out in the Mobile Homes Act. You or the site owner can apply to change the terms of the agreement within six months of the issue of the original written statement. Either side can apply to the County Court or to an arbitrator if they cannot agree the terms. Check that the agreement states the amount of pitch fees you will have to pay and the rules about charging these. If you are unhappy with the arrangements for fees you can, as with the rest of the agreement, apply within six months to change them.

OTHER RIGHTS OF MOBILE HOME OWNERS

You can sell your home and pass on the agreement with the site owner to a person of your choice.[59] You can also give your home to a member of your family. In either case, the new owner must be approved by the site owner, but this approval cannot be unreasonably withheld. If you think the site owner is withholding approval unreasonably you can apply to the court or an arbitrator for an order that the site owner must give approval. If you sell your home the site owner can claim a commission of up to 10 per cent of the price. If you die, members of your family who were living with you will automatically inherit the agreement with the site owner and all your legal rights.

SETTLING DISPUTES

If you have a dispute with the site owner you can settle this by going either to the County Court or to an arbitrator who is an independent person agreed by both sides.[60] Your written agreement may set out the procedure for appointing an arbitrator. You can only use an arbitrator if both you and the site owner have made a written agreement to do so in the event of a dispute. Otherwise you can go to court. Arbitration can be quicker and cheaper than going to court, but make sure it is in your interests before agreeing to it. Once you have made a written agreement to use an arbitrator rather than the court you will be bound by this and you cannot then go to court unless you believe the arbitrator was biased (for example, because he or she was connected with the site owner in some way) or if a mistake was made over the law. If the site owner's proposed written agreement includes the use of arbitration, get advice before signing it.

Squatters

This section is for people who are squatting or thinking of squatting in premises without the permission of the owner. If you have permission from the owner, whether written or spoken, then you may be either a licensee or a tenant and this section does not apply to you. Squatters who do not have the permission of the owner to live in a property count in law as *trespassers*. This is not in itself a crime, but it is easy for the owners to evict you very quickly. There are a number of ways they might do this.

GETTING A POSSESSION ORDER FROM THE COURT

Normally, an owner will go to court to get a possession order to evict you. There are special procedures for evicting squatters quickly. The owner does not even have to give your name to the court. The first you hear may be papers from the court giving you the date of the court hearing. This may give as little as five days' notice. The owner can go either to the County Court or the High Court. If the court decides that you are trespassers, it must grant an immediate possession order, though you may be able to negotiate with the owner for a delay of perhaps two or four weeks if you agree beforehand not to defend the case in court. Owners will normally use the court bailiffs to carry out the eviction and this would give you a further week or so. You should not obstruct the bailiff in any way as this is a criminal offence.[61]

EVICTION BY SOMEONE LIVING IN OR ENTITLED TO LIVE IN THE PROPERTY

Squatters do not usually want to take someone else's home, but if you do find yourself in this position, you could be committing a criminal offence if they ask you to leave and you refuse. The circumstances in which this can happen are set out in the Criminal Law Act 1977.[62] If someone who qualifies as a *displaced residential occupier* or a *protected intending occupier* (or someone acting on behalf of either) asks you to leave and you refuse, you could be prosecuted.

- A *displaced residential occupier* is someone who was living in the property immediately before it was squatted. You would have a defence to any prosecution if you had reasonable grounds for believing that the person had not been living there.

- There are two types of *protected intending occupier:*

  — owners (including long leaseholders) who intend to live in the property themselves. When asking you to leave these people, or their representatives, have to present you with a sworn statement that they come into this category.

  — people who have been offered a tenancy of the property by a public sector landlord such as a local council or housing association. These people, or their representatives, have to present you with a certificate from the landlord that the property has been offered to and accepted by a protected intending occupier. Private landlords cannot use this provision.

FORCIBLE EVICTION OF SQUATTERS

Some owners may use force to evict squatters. If they try to do so they may be committing a criminal offence and you should get advice. However, taking the owner to court will not get you back into the property. Some owners wait until everyone is out and then change the locks on the property. This is not in itself illegal. If you are squatting or thinking of squatting get advice as soon as possible; it may be too late once the owner has started to evict you.

3. Paying for your home and reducing your housing costs

Private tenants

There are a number of ways in which private tenants can reduce their costs and get help with paying for their home:

- If your tenancy began before 15 January 1989 you may be able to get a *fair* or *reasonable rent* registered. Once this is fixed the landlord cannot charge more. First you need to know whether you have *full, restricted* or only *basic* protection as a tenant. See Chapter 2 for advice on this. If you are a *fully protected* regulated tenant, see the next section. If you have *restricted protection* see page 94. If you have only *basic protection* you do not have any rights to get a rent registered.

- If your tenancy began on or after 15 January 1989 and the landlord tries to charge a rent higher than other open market rents in the area you may be able to reduce this to a market rent (see page 95).

- Tenants may be eligible to claim money to help pay their rent and rates through the *housing benefit scheme* (see page 103).

- Tenants have legal rights to challenge unreasonable service charges (see page 96).

FAIR RENTS FOR REGULATED TENANTS

If you are a fully protected regulated tenant (see page 52) you have the right to get a fair rent fixed. This will usually mean that your tenancy began before 15 January 1989. Fair rents are fixed by the *Rent Officer.* Before deciding to apply to the Rent Officer it is very important to find out:

- *Are you certain you are a regulated tenant?* If you are not a regulated tenant the Rent Officer cannot help you and, worse, any attempt to get your rent reduced could lead to you being evicted by the landlord. If you are in any doubt, get advice. If you are a regulated tenant, the landlord cannot evict you because you go to the Rent Officer.

- *What rents has the Rent Officer fixed on similar properties?* The Rent Officer will look at rents fixed on similar properties when deciding what your rent should be. These other rents are known as *comparables*. The Rent Officer can put the rent up as well as down, so it is important to check on other rents before applying. Rent Officers keep a register of rents which is open for public inspection at their offices. Try to find a number of rent registrations on properties which are as close as possible to your own home in terms of neighbourhood, size, amenities, floor level and facilities. Look at the most recent registrations as rents are always increasing. It is very important to remember that **fair rents in the register do not include rates**. Unless you pay rates separately to the council then they will be included, along with rent, in your payments to your landlord. So, to compare your rent with the fair rents registered you will have first to take off the amount paid to your landlord for rates. If you do not know how much the rates on your home are, you can find out from the local council. If comparable rents registered recently are lower than yours it is probably worth applying for a fair rent. Keep a note of the addresses and rents fixed on what seem to be similar properties as these will be useful in presenting your case to the Rent Officer. If you discover a fair rent has already been registered on your home (even if it was before you moved in) and you have been paying more than this (after deducting rates) then you can reclaim the extra amount you have been paying for up to two years after it was paid. If the landlord will not reimburse you, you can go to court to get your money back or deduct it from future rent payments.

Applying to the Rent Officer

If you decide to apply for a fair rent you should get a form from the Rent Officer (the address is in the telephone directory). You will have to give details of the accommodation and the rent you think should be registered. It is best to get help filling in this form from an advice centre. A copy of this completed form will be sent to the landlord who will be asked to say what he or she thinks the rent should be. Similarly, if it is the landlord who makes the application then you will get a copy of it and a chance to state what you think the rent should be. You can also make a joint application with the landlord if you have agreed a rent, although the Rent Officer will still make an independent assessment and could fix a different rent.

Before fixing a rent the Rent Officer will usually visit to inspect your home and either then, or at another date, hold a consultation with you and the landlord to hear both sides. This is an informal hearing and it is not usually necessary to be represented, although you can be if you wish. If the landlord is likely to argue that you are not a regulated tenant and therefore the Rent Officer cannot fix a fair rent, you should get legal advice and you may want to be represented by a solicitor at the hearing. Legal aid is not available, however, to pay for the solicitor's fees for representing you at the hearing, although you may get legal aid for advice before the hearing (see page 166).

In deciding what is a fair fent, the Rent Officer must take account of all the circumstances[1] and in particular the property's age, character, locality, state of repair and the quality and condition of any furniture provided.The Rent Officer is not allowed to take account of the *personal circumstances* of landlord or tenant, so there is no point in arguing that you cannot afford to pay the rent because of your level of income. If this is a problem, see page 103 on claiming housing benefit. The Rent Officer will also disregard any improvements you have made (unless you had to do them under the terms of the tenancy agreement) and any damage or disrepair which is your fault. Before the Rent Officer comes you should make a note of all the things which are inadequate about the property and the neighbourhood. If you do not have a list of furniture agreed with the landlord you should point out to the Rent Officer everything that belongs to you and not the landlord.

The final and most important thing the Rent Officer has to disregard is any *scarcity value* of the property. If your home is in an area where there is a shortage of places to rent, rents which have not been fixed by the Rent Officer will be pushed up because of the large number of people chasing each home. The Rent Officer has to disregard this factor and fix a rent as if there were no shortage of homes in the area.

You should, within a few weeks of the Rent Officer's visit and consultation, receive written notice of the rent registered. This is the fair rent which will be for a two year period. If the rent has been **reduced**, this amount is the most the landlord can charge; it is payable from the date of registration, even if your tenancy agreement states that a higher rent is payable. If the rent has been **increased**, then the landlord may not be able to claim the full increase straight away. There are two reasons for this:

- If you have a *fixed term tenancy* (see page 56), which has not yet run out and the amount of rent agreed is less than the fair rent that has been registered, then the landlord cannot make any increase until the fixed term agreement does run out, unless the tenancy agreement states that he or she can do so.[2]

- Before the landlord can make the increase he or she must give a *notice of increase* in the proper form laid down by law.[3]

Once the rent has been fixed the landlord cannot make any further increases for at least two years except for any increases in rates or variable service charges (see page 96). However, if the property has been greatly improved by the landlord then he or she can apply for a higher rent before the two years are up. But the rent cannot be increased because of improvements made by the tenant. If the property has seriously deteriorated you could apply for a reduction in the rent. The only other circumstance in which a re-registration could be made in less than two years is where the landlord and tenant apply jointly for a new rent.[4]

If either you or the landlord are dissatisfied with the fair rent that has been registered, you can appeal to the Rent Assessment Committee. This appeal normally has to be made within 28 days. **In a high proportion of cases Rent Assessment Committees increase the rent to a higher level than that fixed by the Rent Officer, so it is very inadvisable to appeal unless you are very confident the Rent Officer has made a mistake. Always get advice before deciding to appeal.**

REASONABLE RENTS FOR TENANTS AND LICENSEES WITH RESTRICTED PROTECTION

See page 60 for which tenants have restricted protection. A few licensees also have restricted protection, but for the sake of simplicity they are all referred to as tenants in this section.

Anyone with restricted protection can apply to the Rent Tribunal for a *reasonable rent* to be fixed.[5] However, as all these tenants can be evicted by their landlords, it is highly inadvisable to make an application unless it is with the landlord's agreement, or unless you are anyway planning to leave the accommodation in the next few months or the landlord has already given you Notice to Quit. If you already have a Notice to Quit you have to apply to the Tribunal before the notice expires. Unlike Rent Officers, Rent Tribunals have no guidelines laid down for them and they have a wide degree of discretion over how they decide what is reasonable rent. The landlord or the tenant, or both together, can apply for a rent to be fixed. The Tribunal can increase or reduce the rent, or keep it at its present level. It will be fixed for two years unless there has been a substantial change of circumstances.

You can check in the register kept by the local Rent Assessment Panel whether a rent is already registered on the accommodation; if you discover that a rent was already registered before you moved in and you have been paying more, you can recover the excess from the landlord. Indeed, the landlord has committed a criminal offence by charging more.

If you make an application for a reasonable rent to be fixed you will have to attend a meeting of the Tribunal. This consists of three people and the hearings are fairly informal. The Tribunal members will normally visit the accommodation before the hearing. If you feel you would like someone to speak for you at the hearing contact a local advice agency to see if they can help. If the Tribunal increases the rent there is no need for the landlord to serve any special notice on the tenant and the increase is not phased; it applies straight away, as does any decrease.

RENTS FOR ASSURED TENANTS

If you have an assured tenancy (see page 67) then your landlord can charge a market rent, so there is little that you can do to reduce it. However, the landlord can only increase the rent once a year unless: [6].

- the tenancy is for a fixed term (see page 56 for an explanation of this), **or**
- if it had previously been a fixed term tenancy and the landlord has not renewed it, **or**
- the tenancy agreement states that the rent can be increased at an earlier date.

If none of these conditions apply, then the landlord may serve a notice on the tenant that a new rent will apply no earlier than one year after the tenancy began plus a minimum period after the notice has been served. This minimum period must be at least a month if the rent is paid monthly or more often. If the rent is paid less frequently, then the notice period must be equal to the period for which rent is paid. In the unlikely event of rent only being paid yearly, then the period of notice is six months. The landlord can only serve such a notice once a year.

If you do not agree with the rent increase proposed by the landlord you can apply to the local Rent Assessment Committee for a rent to be fixed. They will fix a rent that they think the landlord could get on the open market, disregarding any increase in value brought about by the tenants' own improvements to the property or any decrease in value brought about by the tenant breaking the tenancy agreement. The rent they fix will not include service charges (see page 96) or rates. Since the Rent Assessment Committee will fix the rent at a market level, there is likely to be little benefit in applying to them, unless you are certain that the landlord will not be able to evict you (see pages 67) and the landlord is trying to exploit your wish to stay in your home by demanding a higher rent than he or she could otherwise get on the open market.

RENTS FOR ASSURED SHORTHOLD TENANTS

If you have an assured shorthold tenancy (see page 71), then the landlord is entitled to charge a market rent on the property and there is likely to be little you can do to reduce it. If, however, you believe that the rent is significantly higher than those charged for similar properties on the open market in the same area, then you can apply to the local Rent Assessment Committee who will decide what a market rent should be.[7] They will, however, only do this if there are a sufficient number of similar lettings in the area for them to make a decision. This is unlikely to be of much assistance to you, unless you were somehow tricked at the beginning of the tenancy into paying a much higher rent than the landlord could otherwise have got on the open market and you do not mind increasing the likelihood of losing the tenancy when the shorthold agreement comes to an end.

SERVICE CHARGES IN FLATS FOR PRIVATE AND HOUSING ASSOCIATION TENANTS AND OWNER OCCUPIERS WITH LONG LEASES

Private and housing association tenants and owners of long leases of flats often have to pay a service charge to cover repairs to the block and provision of common services such as cleaning. In this section all are referred to as 'tenants'.

If you are a tenant who is fully protected by the Rent Act 1977 (see page 52) or a housing association tenant and you have a fair rent fixed by the Rent Officer (see page 100) then check whether the Rent Officer has included in that fair rent the cost of services. If the cost of services is not included, or if you do not have a fair rent registered, or you are an owner occupier with a long lease, then the amount of service charge the landlord can recover from you is controlled by the Landlord and Tenant Acts 1985 and 1987.[8] Before any major repair work is carried out you have a right to be consulted over the nature and cost of the work. You have a *right to information* from the landlord on how service charges are made up and a *right to challenge unreasonable charges*.

The right to be consulted

If the landlord wants to carry out major building work you have a right to be consulted in advance if it is likely to cost more than a certain amount, known as the *prescribed amount*. At present the prescribed amount is £50 multiplied by the number of flats in the building or £1000, whichever is the greater. The landlord must get at least two estimates for the work, at least one of them from a firm unconnected with the landlord. He or she must then give all the tenants who might have to pay the cost a notice describing the work to be done and copies of the estimates. The notice must give an address to which comments can be sent and a closing date for these comments. At least one month must be allowed for comments unless the work is urgent. As an alternative to sending the separate notices to the tenants the landlord can display copies in a prominent place in the building.

If the work is of a kind which your lease states the landlord can carry out, then you cannot usually prevent it from being carried out. However, if your lease does not authorise the landlord to carry out that kind of work then you cannot be charged for it.

If you think the estimates are too expensive you can get your own estimate and send it to the landlord . If the landlord does not consult you in advance or does not give you the correct period in which to comment then you could take the landlord to the County Court. If the court finds in your favour the landlord will not normally be able to charge any more than the prescribed amount (i.e. £50 per flat or £1000 divided by the number of flats, whichever is the greater). Alternatively, you could simply pay only the prescribed amount and then it is up to the landlord to take you to court to try to recover the excess amount. However, if the landlord cannot go through the proper consultation procedures for good reason (for example the work has to be carried out in an emergency) you may still have to pay your full share of the cost.

The right to information on service charges

You have a right to a summary of what the landlord has spent to make up your service charge. You are entitled to ask for this for any one year, which may be the landlord's accounting year or the past 12 months. Once you have made your request in writing the landlord must provide you with a summary of costs within one month, or six months of the end of the period covered by the summary, whichever is the later. If the summary does not give you enough information you have a right to inspect the landlord's accounts and receipts.

If you do not know how to contact your landlord you can give a written request to the person who collects the rent who must then send it to the landlord. If your landlord refuses to provide this information the local council can prosecute him or her.

The right to challenge unreasonable charges

If you think you should not have to pay a particular service charge, or if you think it is too high, tell your landlord or the agent. If you cannot reach agreement with the landlord you have two possible courses of action. You could take the landlord to the County Court, which will decide whether you have to pay and if so, how much, or you could pay the amount you think is reasonable and then the landlord will have to take you to court if he or she disagrees.

The landlord can only charge in advance for services if this is allowed for in your lease and then can only make reasonable advance charges.

Unreasonable charges can again be challenged in the County Court. If the work turns out to cost less than the advance payment, the landlord must repay the difference or deduct that amount from future service charges. The landlord cannot charge for costs incurred more than 18 months before a demand for payment unless he or she has informed you within 18 months that the costs had been incurred and that a service charge demand would follow.

Insurance

Tenants can require their landlord to provide details of the insurance policy on their building. Within one month the landlord must provide a copy of the policy or a summary of it. Within six months of receiving these details, tenants can require the landlord to allow them to inspect the full policy and details of payments.

Action through a tenants' association

Challenging service charges can be difficult for individual tenants. You could be much more effective by getting together with others to form a tenants' association or joining one if it already exists. Tenants' associations with a sufficient number of members have a right to be recognised by the landlord. Recognised tenants' associations have the same legal rights as individual tenants and some additional rights. They also have a better chance of being able to enforce these rights by acting together.

The main additional rights enjoyed by tenants' associations are over consultation on the employment of managing agents. A recognised tenants' association can require the landlord to provide details of managing agents and can comment on their brief and performance. Once such a notice has been served the landlord must inform the tenants' association of any proposal to change the managing agent, inform the association at least once every five years of any changes since the last notice, and invite comments on the agents and on whether they should be retained. The landlord must have regard to any comments made by the association about managing agents.

If the landlord refuses to give written notice of recognition to your association you can apply to the local Rent Assessment Panel (the address is in the telephone directory) for a *certificate of recognition.* There are no formal rules on what associations should be given recognition, but government guidelines suggest normally 60 per cent of tenants of flats in the block should belong to the association, although in some circumstances more than one association might be recognised. The Rent Assessment Panel can advise you on what you need to do to gain a certificate of recognition.

For futher information on the rights of long leaseholders see the SHAC guide *Owning your flat* (see *Useful publications*).

Council Tenants

RENTS

Local councils are entitled in law to fix their own rents. The rents are supposed to be reasonable,[9] but this leaves a very wide scope and it is extremely unlikely that a council's rent levels would be successfully challenged in the courts. Council tenants, like other tenants, can claim housing benefit to meet the cost of rent and rates (see page 103).

RENT ARREARS

If you have difficulty in paying the rent and get into arrears you could risk losing your home. So if you have money problems contact the local council immediately and tell it why. Get independent advice as well so that you can check:

- ○ Can you get help with paying the rent by claiming housing benefit? If you are already getting housing benefit, are you receiving the right amount? (See page 100.)

- ○ Are you getting the other welfare benefits to which you are entitled? There are a large number of benefits available, whether you are working or not working. (See *Useful publications.)*

Do not stop paying the rent because the council is failing to do repairs. Instead, see page 133 on how to force it to do the repairs.

If you have money problems discuss them with the housing department as soon as possible. If the council takes you to court to evict you for rent arrears it may still be possible to save your home. Try to work out how you can pay off the arrears over a period of time, but make sure than any agreement you reach with the council on this is one that you can afford to keep.

If you have got problems over paying the rent, or if you or your partner have run up rent arrears, the sooner you get advice the more chance you will have of saving your home.

'Distraint' or 'distress' for rent arrears

Some councils resort to an ancient common law right which enables them to seize people's possessions and sell them to pay off debts such as rent arrears without even getting a court order. This is known as *'distraint'* or *'distress'*. However, the council may break the law if it fails to seize the goods in the correct manner. If you are threatened with this, get advice immediately.

Housing association tenants

RENTS

Rents for housing association tenants depend on whether the tenancy began before or after 15 January 1989. **Tenancies which began before that date** have *fair rents* fixed in the same way as for regulated private tenants (see page 91). The housing association will automatically apply for a fair rent to be fixed, so there is no need for the tenant to take any action. As housing associations are non-profit making bodies they do not have the same incentive as private landlords to try to increase tenants' rents, but you can still make any representations you wish to the Rent Officer. Tenancies which begin on or after 15 January 1989 will be **assured tenancies** with very little legal control over rent levels (see page 95). Help with paying the rent is available through the housing benefit scheme run by the local council (see page 103).

RENT ARREARS

Housing association tenants with difficulties in paying their rent are in much the same positon as council tenants (see page 99). However, unlike councils, housing associations are not able to use the procedure of distraint to seize people's possessions without going to court first. As a result its use is virtually unknown by non-council landlords.

Home Owners

CHOOSING THE RIGHT MORTGAGE

Mortgage costs can vary widely depending on the type of loan you have and the type of lender you borrow from. See page 34 for advice on the best value in mortgages.

TAX RELIEF ON MORTGAGE INTEREST PAYMENTS

The largest subsidy available to any group of people for help with housing cost is tax relief for home owners. Any money you pay in mortgage interest can be set against your taxable income. If, for example, you pay £1,000 a year interest on your mortgage you can pay this out of tax free income. At the basic rate of tax of 25 per cent you would normally pay £250 tax on £1,000 income. But if this money is spent on mortgage interest payments you pay no tax, saving yourself £250 and in effect only paying £750 for every £1,000 worth of interest payments. Wealthier people who pay higher rates of tax do even better. Someone paying tax at 40 per cent will only pay £600 for every £1000 worth of interest payments. You can claim this tax relief for the first £30,000 of your mortgage loan.

THE HOMELOAN SCHEME

This government scheme offers a small amount of extra money for first time buyers who have saved for two years before applying for a mortgage. Savings can be with a building society, bank or National Savings Scheme. You have to register with the organisation with which you are saving by filling in a homeloan scheme form available from them. You must have £600 in the account when you claim and an average of at least £300 over the past 12 months. You must also be buying a home which costs less than an amount fixed for each region. The benefits are fairly small; an extra grant of between £40 and £110 and an extra loan of £600 on which you do not have to make any repayments for the first five years. You can get further details from your bank or building society.

IF YOU ARE NOT WORKING OR WORK LESS THAN 24 HOURS A WEEK

If you are not in paid work or work less than 24 hours a week, have a very low or no income, and do not have more than £6,000 in savings, you may be entitled to claim *income support*. Get advice if you think you might be eligible. If you do qualify the Department of Social Security (DSS) will pay:

- Mortgage interest payments. They will usually only pay the interest on the loan taken out to buy the home, but they can also pay interest on a loan taken out for major repairs or improvements. They will not repay the capital part of the mortgage loan or insurance premiums for an endowment mortgage. If you and your partner are aged under 60, you will normally only receive a half of your mortgage interest payments for the first 16 weeks of your claim. After that interest payments should be met in full. If you have had to start claiming from the DSS and cannot afford to keep up your full mortgage repayments, see *Cutting mortgage costs* below;
- An allowance for repairs and insurance;
- water rates;

- ground rent if you are a long leaseholder;
- other service and maintenance charges for long leaseholders.

The DSS should also notify the local council that you are entitled to receive housing benefit to help pay your rates (see page 103).

CUTTING MORTGAGE COSTS

If you are having difficulties repaying your mortgage there are a number of ways you can consider reducing your costs. What you can do depends on the number and type of mortgages you have. See page 34 for a description of the different types of mortgage.

If you have a capital repayment mortgage

If you have only one loan and it is a capital repayment mortgage, you can ask your lender to accept payment of interest only and to allow you to put off paying back any capital. You may particularly need to consider this if you are on income support as the DSS will only pay the interest part of a mortgage. If this is not possible you could, as an alternative, ask your lender to extend the period of the mortgage (say from 20 to 25 years), as this will reduce your payments.

If you have an endowment mortgage

If you have only one loan and if it is an endowment mortgage you could consider changing to a capital repayment mortgage as this is often cheaper. You will need to get your lender to agree to this.

You could also ask your lender to agree to let you pay interest only on the loan and to stop paying the insurance policy premiums which go towards paying off the capital. Again, this will be particularly important if you are getting income support as the DSS will only pay for interest charges. However, many insurance policies are automatically cancelled if a certain number of premiums are not paid (for example six months' premiums), so your lender may only agree to this for a very short period.

If you have two or more mortgages

If you have more than one mortgage and are paying higher interest on one or more of them you can try to rearrange all your borrowing on the cheapest basis. This will probably mean an ordinary capital repayment mortgage over a long period. If you have your first mortgage with a building society or major bank ask them for help with a remortgage in this way. Alternatively, ask your local council for help with a remortgage if:

- your first mortgage is with that council, **or**

- your first mortgage is with a finance company or fringe bank, **or**
- your building society refuses to offer a remortgage or you are in danger of losing your home.

Do not go to a finance company or fringe bank for a remortgage as they will probably charge high interest rates.

Home owners on low incomes, whether they are working or not, can also claim help in paying rates through the housing benefit scheme (see below).

MORTGAGE ARREARS

If you have problems in keeping up with your mortgage payments and get into arrears, your lender could eventually get you evicted and sell the property to recover their loan.

But even if you have got into arrears there are many things you can do. Get advice immediately and check:

- Can you reduce your mortgage costs? (see page 102)
- Can you get extra help with paying the mortgage and other costs? (see page 100)
- Are you getting all the welfare benefits to which you are entitled? There are a large number of benefits available, whether you are working or not.
- Could you claim a grant from the local authority to help with repairs or improvements? (see page 138)

If you have difficulty in keeping up payments get in touch with your lender immediately and explain your difficulties. There are many ways of keeping your home; for more detailed advice see the SHAC/CPAG book *Rights Guide for Home Owners* (see *Useful publications)*.

SERVICE CHARGES IN FLATS

If you have bought a long lease on a flat and have to pay service charges see page 96 for details of legal controls over these.

Housing benefit

Housing benefit is the name of the government scheme for helping people meet the cost of their rent and rates. A new scheme was introduced in April 1988.

The scheme is extremely complicated. This section explains its main features but does not cover all the details. If you have further questions get advice and see also *Useful publications* for more detailed guides available from SHAC.

Around one in three households in Britain qualify for housing benefit. Private and housing association tenants can claim a *rent allowance*, council tenants can claim a *rent rebate*, and all types of occupiers — tenants and home owners — can claim a *rate rebate* for help with paying the rates. The figures at the end of this section will help you to work out whether you are likely to qualify. Housing benefit is usually paid by the local council.

The way to claim depends on whether or not you are eligible for income support from the DSS. If you are receiving income support (or think you may be eligible to receive it), read on. If you are not eligible for income support turn to the section headed: *People not on income support: rent allowances, rent rebates and rate rebates* on page 105. General points affecting everybody who gets housing benefit are dealt with on page 107.

PEOPLE ON INCOME SUPPORT

If you qualify for income support you should get a housing benefit claim form along with your income support claim form from the DSS. The DSS should then send your housing benefit form onto the local council. If you are a council tenant or home owner the council will then work out your benefit. If you are a private or housing association tenant you will have to fill in an additional form giving details of your tenancy, the amount of rent and rates you pay and the number of people living in your household. If you have a subtenant you will also have to give details of any income received from the subtenant.

If you are living in a bed and breakfast hotel or accommodation where you get food as well as lodging you will not qualify for housing benefit. But if you live in a hostel, you will instead get a board and lodging allowance added to your income support by the DSS (see page 113).

You should normally receive the **full cost** of your rent and 80 per cent of your rates from the council. However, in certain circumstances deductions are made. These deductions are:

- If you have *subtentants, lodgers* or people who count as *non-dependants*[10] (for example children over 18 who have left school or elderly relatives) living with you, there will be a deduction from your benefit to take account of the contribution these people are assumed to make to your housing costs.

If you have a subtenant this will normally be the amount you receive from the subtenant towards the rent and rates that you pay less £4, or £11.00 if the subtenant pays for heating. If you have lodgers or non-dependants a fixed sum is deducted depending on their age and circumstances. (These fixed deductions are listed on page 110.)

- If you are a tenant and have to pay service charges for the provision of *common services* such as caretaking, communal rooms, or warders for the elderly and disabled, most of these charges are eligible for benefit.[11] However, payments for *personal services* provided to you such as personal laundry or meals, are not eligible for benefit and the cost of these is deducted before calculating your housing benefit.

- *Water rates* are not eligible for housing benefit.

Tenants: heating and other fuel charges

These charges are not covered by housing benefit. But if you are a private or housing association tenant and the charge which is included in your rent is not readily identifiable, then the following fixed amounts are set as being not eligible for housing benefit:[12]

Heating	£7.00 a week
Hot water	£0.85 a week
Cooking	£0.85 a week
Lighting	£0.55 a week

These are reduced if you occupy only one room. You can also provide evidence to the local authority asking them to reduce these deductions if you think they are too high.

If you have no control over the fuel charges you have to pay and you are on income support then you should not have more than £3.00 in excess of the fixed amounts above counted in the calculation of your housing benefit.

People receiving income support should now turn to page 107.

PEOPLE NOT ON INCOME SUPPORT FROM DSS: RENT ALLOWANCES, RENT REBATES AND RATE REBATES

Rent

Tenants and licensees are eligible for housing benefit for accommodation which they occupy as their home. This includes people living in hostels and mobile homes.[13] (If you live in a hostel, hotel or lodgings see page 113 for additional rules which might apply to you.)

Rent allowances and rent rebates are assessed on the actual rent you pay your landlord, including any charge for furniture if you rent furnished accommodation.[14] If a fair rent or reasonable rent has been registered (see page 91) these are normally the maximum amounts on which you can get an allowance.[15] Charges for most services such as caretaking, communal rooms and warden services for the elderly or disabled will generally be included too, provided you have to pay the charge as a condition of your tenancy.[16] But payments for meals and for amenities like heat and light are not included.

Tenants, licensees and home owners are eligible for *rate rebates*. Rate rebates are assessed on the rates paid to the council, whether you pay these directly or with your rent. Water rates, which include charges for water, sewerage and environmental services, are not covered by rate rebates.

The council may make a reduction in the rent and rates eligible for benefit if it believes that your housing is unreasonably large or the rent is unreasonably high, and it may reduce the rates eligible for benefit if it thinks that your home is in an unnecessarily expensive area.[17] If it does reduce your benefit you can appeal against the decision (see page 108). If your landlord is a housing association, the association may be able to help you with an appeal.

How rent allowances, rent rebates and rate rebates are calculated
To claim housing benefit you have to fill out a form provided by the local council. To assess whether you are entitled to a rent allowance or rent and rate rebate, the council will need to know:

- How many people are living in your home and whether they are related to you. Families and couples who live together are usually assessed together, but unrelated people sharing a home who are not married or living together should be assessed individually.[18]

- Your income and that of your husband, wife or partner. This will normally be based on your last five weeks' net earnings, after tax, if you are paid weekly, or two months' net earnings, after tax, if you are paid monthly. You will probably be asked to produce pay slips or other proof of earnings. If you are self-employed the assessment is made on your net profits after income tax and national insurance. Income other than earnings, including pensions and state benefits such as child benefit and income from investments, is taken into account. But certain amounts of income are disregarded. These are known as *income disregards*. All of them are deducted from your income before any calculation of benefit.

Having assessed the income which it will take into account, the council will then work out your applicable amount, a figure set each year by the government, which is designed to reflect your basic living costs and which increases with your family size. The applicable amounts are listed on page 111. Lone parents, handicapped people and people over retirement age receive an increased applicable amount.

The next step is to work out your maximum housing benefit. This figure is worked out as 100 per cent of your rent and 80 per cent of your rates. Next, the council will compare your *income* with your applicable amount.

- If your income is less than or equal to the applicable amount then you are entitled to the maximum housing benefit.

- If your income is **above** the applicable amount the housing benefit you get is **reduced** from the maximum level (see page 113 for an example).

Deductions may also be made for non-dependants or subtenants in the same way as for people on income support (see page 113).

ALL CLAIMANTS: HOW HOUSING BENEFIT IS PAID

The council should give you a written statement of how much benefit you are entitled to receive within 14 days of getting a completed application form from you or from the DSS if you are getting income support.[19] If, for any reason, your application form did not contain all the information needed to make the assessment, the council can ask you for the necessary extra information and then have a further 14 days within which it should tell you how much benefit you will receive.

For *council tenants* the amount of your rent rebate is deducted from the rent you pay.

For *private and housing association tenants* the rent allowance is paid directly to you, usually by Giro or cheque, but you can ask for other arrangements if those do not suit you. The council can decide to make this payment on a monthly or fortnightly basis but you can insist on a fortnightly payment if you are getting a rent allowance of over £2 a week.[20] Your benefit should be paid to you, not to your landlord, but it can be paid directly to the landlord if you ask for or agree to it being paid in this way. If you are a tenant and you owe more than 8 weeks' rent the landlord can ask for your benefit to be paid directly to him or her.[21]

If you pay your *rates* directly to the council then your rate rebate will normally be deducted from what you pay. If you pay rates together with your rent to a private landlord or housing association then the rate rebate will be paid to you together with your rent allowance.

HOW LONG HOUSING BENEFIT LASTS

If you are on income support then your housing benefit will continue as long as your entitlement to income support, but you will have to fill in a fresh claim form usually each year. If you are a private or housing association tenant and your rent or rates go up, you should tell the council immediately as you will probably be entitled to more benefit.

If you come off income support you may still qualify for housing benefit, depending on your new level of income. Notify the council immediately of this or any other change in your circumstances which might affect your entitlement to benefit.

If you are not getting income support but are getting housing benefit, then this benefit will be reassessed regularly. It will normally last for a maximum of 60 weeks before being reassessed by the council.[22]

IF YOU ARE AWAY FROM HOME[23]

You can still get housing benefit if you are away from home for a while; for example, on holiday, looking for a job elsewhere, in hospital or in prison, providing you still have to pay rent and rates on your home. Benefit can be paid for periods of up to one year's absence from home at the discretion of the local council.

Normally, you can only get benefit on one home. There are, however, two exceptions:

- If you are obliged to make payments for two homes at the same time (for example because you are moving home) you may get housing benefit on both for a period of up to 28 days.

- If you have to make payments for two homes at the same time because you have left one through fear of violence, you may get housing benefit on both for an indefinite period.

APPEALING AGAINST THE ASSESSMENT OF HOUSING BENEFIT

If you think there has been a mistake in assessing your entitlement you have a right to appeal. If you are considering appealing then get independent advice to help you do so. The procedure works as follows:[24]

- If you do not agree with the council's assessment you should ask for a fuller explanation showing how your claim was assessed. Write to the council and keep a copy of the letter. The council should send you a full written explanation within 14 days.

- If you are still not satisfied, write to the council explaining why. You must do this within six weeks of receiving the council's first assessment, and let you know, within two weeks and in writing, whether the original assessment is confirmed or altered.

- If you are still not satisfied, you can appeal to a special review board of local councillors. Your appeal must be made in writing, explaining why you disagree and where you think the council's decision is wrong. You must do this within 28 days of the council's review of its decision. The appeal should be heard within six weeks. You are entitled to attend and also to be accompanied or represented by someone else. If your appeal is successful the decision is backdated to the date of your application.

If your appeal is unsuccessful and you still think the council is wrong, it may be possible to take the case to court or to complain to the Ombudsman. If you are thinking of doing either of these things it is important that you get further independent advice as soon as possible. The case can only be taken to court if you consider that the review board has wrongly interpreted the law or failed to take account of all the facts, or reached its decision unreasonably or in an improper manner.

SPECIAL ARRANGEMENTS FOR STUDENTS

Most students are entitled to claim housing benefit on accommodation they are living in as their home, even if they only occupy it during term-time.[25] However, students living in halls of residence and other accommodation for which they pay rent to their university, polytechnic or college are not entitled to claim housing benefit. Overseas students from countries which are not members of the EEC or which have not signed reciprocal agreements with the UK are not entitled to housing benefit. There are special rules concerning this and if you are in any doubt, get advice.

Generally, students are assessed in the same way as other applicants, but some special rules apply. The most important of these are:

- A fixed amount is deducted from a student's eligible rent during the period of study (£18.50 a week in London, £14.00 a week outside London). This rule applies in all standard housing benefit cases where the student is studying full time, as well as to eligible overseas students, **whether or not a grant has been awarded**.

  Although the above amounts are also disregarded from a student's income, again whatever its source, in the benefit assessment the net effect of this rule is to reduce, and sometimes eliminate entirely, an eligible student's housing benefit.

- The above rule only applies during the period of study which for most students will include the Christmas and Easter vacations as well as term-time but not, in most cases, the summer vacation.

- All items of a student's income are taken into account in making the benefit assessment, including any assessed parental or spouses' contribution to the grant whether paid in full or not at all.

  Some special types of grant income are also disregarded. The balance of income is then apportioned over the number of weeks in the period of study to arrive at weekly income for benefit purposes.

- Students are not eligible for housing benefit for accommodation which they are absent from outside the period of study.

There are a number of other detailed rules affecting a student's entitlement to housing benefit, so you should get further advice if you are in any doubt. Your best source of advice will be your Student Union or your college's Accommodation or Welfare Service.

HOUSING BENEFIT: THE FIGURES

Some of the main figures used in assessing benefit. These rates are regularly changed, generally in April of each year.

1. Deductions for non-dependants

Where non-dependants are:	**Rent**	**Rates**
Not in paid work or a boarder:		
Aged under 18	no deduction	
Aged 18-25 and on income support	—	£3.35
Aged 18 or more	£3.85	£3.35
In paid work or a boarder:		
Aged 18 or more	£9.15	£3.35

Note i) Non-dependant couples are treated as single people — only one deduction is made not two.

ii) Non-dependants in paid work but on low incomes (less than £52.10 a week gross) are treated the same as people not in paid work.

2. Applicable amounts

Personal allowances:

Single claimant:	
aged under 18	£20.80
aged 18-24 inclusive	£27.40
aged 25+	£34.90
Lone parent:	
aged under 18	£20.80
aged 18+	£34.90
Couple:	
both aged under 18	£41.60
at least one aged 18+	£54.80

Addition for each child or young person (dependants' allowances)	
aged under 11	£11.75
aged 11 to 15 inclusive	£17.35
aged 16 or 17	£20.80
aged 18	£27.40
Premiums:	
Any or all of the following:	
Family premium	£6.50
Disabled child premium	
for each qualifying child or young person	£6.50
Severe disability premium	
Single claimant, lone parent	£26.20
Couple (one qualifying)	£26.20
Couple (both qualifying)	£52.40
plus only the most valuable of the following:	
Lone parent premium	£8.60
(NB: for income support, DSS use a premium of £3.90)	
Pensioner premium (aged 60+)	
Single claimant	£11.20
Couple (one or both qualifying)	£17.05
Disability premium (Defined as disabled and under 60) or Higher pensioner premium (Aged 80+ OR defined as disabled and aged 60+):	
Single claimant or lone parent	£13.70
Couple (one or both qualifying)	£19.50

Examples

Income below applicable amount

A claimant's eligible rent is £40.00, and eligible rates are £10.00. Her assessed income is below her applicable amount.

The claimant is therefore entitled to maximum HB in her case:

HB for rent: 100% of eligible rent	£40.00
HB for rates: 80% of eligible rates	£8.00
Total HB	£48.00

The claimant has to find £2.00 per week to pay towards her rates.

Non-dependant joins the household

A non-dependant joins the household of the same claimant, and the higher rate of non-dependant deduction applies.

The claimant is entitled to the maximum HB in her case, but this now involves a non-dependant deduction:

HB for rent:		
100% of eligible rent	£40.00	
Less non-dependant deduction for rent	−£9.15	£30.85
HB for rates:		
80% of eligible rates	£8.00	
Less non-dependant deduction for rates	−£3.45	£4.55
Total HB		£35.40

The claimant has to find £14.60 per week towards her rent and rates, of which she is expected to collect £12.60 from her non-dependant.

Income above applicable amount

A claimant has eligible rent of £20.00 and eligible rates of £7.00. His assessed income is £10.00 above his applicable amount.

Entitlement to housing benefit is therefore:

HB for rent:

100% of eligible rent	£20.00	
Less taper adjustment: 65% of £10.00	−£6.50	£13.50

HB for rates:

80% of eligible rates	£5.60	
Less taper adjustment: 20% of £10.00	−£2.00	£3.60
Total HB		£17.10

So the claimant has to find £9.90 per week towards his rent and rates.

Home owners

Similar examples would apply in the case of a home owner, though excluding, of course, the figures and calculations relating to rent.

People not on income support: how much you will get

The tables on the preceding pages give you an idea of how much housing benefit you may get. (People receiving income support should normally have all their rent and 80% of their rates paid.)

To work out your *weekly income* figure, take your average pay and that of your partner, both after deductions but include overtime, pensions, child benefit and family income supplement.

To work out your *rent*, take your weekly rent, not including rates or any payments for heating or services.

PEOPLE IN HOSTELS, BED AND BREAKFAST HOTELS AND LODGING HOUSES

If your home is in a hostel, a bed and breakfast hotel or in accommodation where you get food and lodging, you can get help with your housing costs. Where to go for help depends on whether or not you are eligible for income support from DSS. If you do not know whether or not you are eligible for income support, get advice and see *Useful publications*.

If you are not eligible for income support from DSS

If you are not eligible for income support then you can claim housing benefit to help with the rent on any type of accommodation which you *occupy as your home.*[26] Your home is defined as your *normal residence*, regardless of how long you have lived there. A hostel can count as a normal residence. There can be difficulties, though, in sorting out how much of the hostel charge is payable for rent and therefore eligible for housing benefit and how much is for elements such as food, which do not count in calculating housing benefit. If you believe this has been wrongly calculated, get advice.

If you are eligible for income support from DSS

If you are receiving income support then you should get a board and lodging allowance until April 1989. After that date claimants living in board and lodging accommodation will need to apply for housing benefit. People living in hostels, residential care homes and nursing homes will continue to have their housing costs met by the DSS for the present. Your total income support will be made up of two elements:

- your board and lodging allowance;
- an allowance for personal expenses.

PEOPLE WITH NO HOME AT ALL

If you have absolutely nowhere to live, the DSS should still pay you benefit and money for somewhere to stay. This could include:

- a voucher for a local lodging house;
- sending you to a *resettlement unit*. These used to be known as reception centres and are intended to help homeless people re-establish themselves. You should not be sent to a resettlement unit just because you are homeless, but only if you can benefit from the help they offer. Your full board and accommodation are paid for.

A SPECIAL NOTE FOR PEOPLE FROM ABROAD

There are certain groups of people who, because of their nationality or immigration status, may lose their right to stay in the country if they claim certain benefits. The rules governing this are extremely complicated and if you are at all unsure of whether to claim benefit, get advice immediately. If you do claim certain benefits when you are prohibited from claiming because of your nationality or immigration status, you may jeopardise your stay in this country and risk deportation.

4: Improving conditions in your home: repairs, improvements and overcrowding

Private and housing association tenants

In almost all cases, private and housing association landlords are legally responsible for repairs to the houses of their tenants. Tenants have a right to repairs under a number of different Acts of Parliament and also under common law. Your tenancy agreement may also set out your rights to get repairs done although it cannot transfer to you any obligations to do repairs which are, in law, the landlord's responsibility. So you should always check on your other legal rights in addition to looking at the tenancy agreement. The first part of this section gives an outline of these legal rights and the second part gives advice on how to enforce them.

LEGAL RIGHTS TO REPAIR

Whose responsibility?

Section 11 of the Landlord and Tenant Act 1985 sets down a comprehensive list of repairs which are always the landlord's responsibility. This covers almost all tenancies. The only exceptions are where:

- the tenancy began before 24 October 1961, **or**
- the lease you originally agreed was for a fixed term of more than seven years.

The Act states that the landlord has to repair the structure, exterior and installations of the dwelling. This includes:

- repairs to the structure such as roof, walls, floors and windows;

- upkeep of the outside of the building including gutters, pipes and drains;
- repair of plumbing and sanitary conveniences such as baths, toilets, sinks and basins;
- repair of installations such as electrical wiring, gas piping, fixed heaters and water heaters.

These are by law your landlord's responsibility **even if your tenancy agreement states that they are not.**

However, this does not require the landlord to rebuild or restore property destroyed by fire or flood.

Local councils' powers and duties

Local councils have a wide range of legal powers and duties to require landlords to do repairs. These powers are set down in the Public Health Acts of 1936 and 1961 and the Housing Act 1985. The next section describes the powers under the Public Health Acts and the following section the powers under the Housing Act. Local councils can and should, if necessary, use powers under both Public Health Acts and the Housing Act at the same time. As a general rule, their powers under the Housing Act are more comprehensive than under Public Health legislation.

Local councils' powers under the Public Health Acts

Councils can use these powers when the property is in such a state as to be a *statutory nuisance*. This is defined as 'any premises in such a state as to be prejudicial to health or a nuisance'.[1] This usually means that the fault is likely to affect your health and safety. Examples of the types of fault covered by this are:

- dampness
- leaking roof
- broken bannisters
- rotten floorboards
- piles of rubbish
- dangerous wiring
- falling slates
- rotten window frames.

If the council is satisfied that there is such a *statutory nuisance* it **must** serve a notice known as an *abatement notice* on the person responsible.[2] This orders the repairs to be done and gives a time by which the work must be finished. If the time limit runs out and the repair has still not been done, the council must apply to the Magistrates' Court for an order against the landlord.[3] The magistrate can order the landlord to do repairs and may impose a fine of up to £2,000. You could also make a separate application to be awarded compensation of up to £2,000 if you can show that you have suffered injury or your property has been damaged because the repairs were not done. If the landlord still does not do the repairs he or she can be fined up to £1,000 with a further fine of £50 a day for every day that the work is not done after the notice has expired. However, these are the maximum fines and it is very unusual for them to be this high. Finally, the council can do the repairs in default and claim the cost from the landlord. However, the council does not have to take this final step if it does not wish to. This can all take a very long time; nine months is not unusual. If there is an urgent need for repairs, for example if your roof is leaking and the ceiling is likely to collapse, the council can serve on the landlord a *Nine Day Notice*.[4] This states that the council will do the work itself giving at least nine days' notice. The landlord can notify the council within seven days that he or she will do the repairs, but the council can still step in if the repairs are not started within a reasonable time. However, even this emergency procedure can take a long time.

There are special arrangements to clear blocked drains and toilets within two days. The council can serve a notice on the landlord giving 48 hours for them to be unblocked.[5] If they are not, the council can do the work and charge the landlord the costs.

There are two main problems with using Public Health Act powers. First, many of the procedures are very lengthy and time-consuming for the local council. Many councils do not use the powers as fully as they could. This can mean that there are long delays, often of many months, or even that the work is not done at all. The second problem is that under the Public Health Acts all the landlord has to do is to stop the immediate problem and the likelihood of it recurring. This could mean, for example, merely replacing damp plaster rather than installing a damp-proof course. Underlying defects may be ignored. So, for example, if there is a leaking roof this may just be patched up rather than properly repaired. However, if the problem is likely to return the local council can serve another notice under the Public Health (Recurring Nuisances) Act 1969 which can order the landlord to do a better job to prevent the problem repeating itself.

Local councils' powers and duties under the Housing Acts

Local councils have extensive powers under the Housing Acts to take action over disrepair. These cover not only properties in very bad condition but also those where the repairs necessary are relatively minor.

If the house is in such bad condition that it is *unfit* for human habitation the council can use its powers to ensure either that the property is made fit or that it is closed (meaning that no one is allowed to live in it) or that it is demolished.

Unfit properties

In deciding whether a house is unfit the council has to consider the following factors:[6]

- *Repair:* for example, where the windows, floors or stairs are defective.
- *Stability:* for example, where there are defects in the structure of the house.
- *Freedom from damp:* for example, where there is rising damp or a leaking roof.
- *Internal arrangement:* for example, a toilet leading directly off a kitchen.
- *Natural lighting:* for example where there are rooms without windows or where light is blocked by other buildings.
- *Ventilation.*
- *Water supply:* where there is no running water or it is polluted.
- *Drainage and sanitary conveniences:* where plumbing, drains or the toilet are inadequate.
- *Facilities for preparation and cooking of food and disposal of waste water:* for example, where there is no proper sink or way of preparing food hygienically.

If the Environmental Health Officer decides that your home is unfit then the normal course of action is for the council to serve a notice on the landlord ordering that the necessary work is done to make the property fit to live in. If, however, this work cannot be done at *reasonable expense* then the local council may require that the house is demolished, or that it is closed, meaning that no one is allowed to live in it.

If the property is unfit and can be repaired at reasonable expense[7]

The council must serve a notice on the landlord stating what work is necessary and giving a time limit for starting and finishing the work. If the landlord disagrees with this notice, he or she can appeal within 21 days to the County Court to have it changed or quashed altogether. If the landlord does not do the work ordered in the notice then the local council may (but does not have to) go in and do the work itself, charging the cost to the landlord. The council can also prosecute the landlord who can be fined.

If the property cannot be made fit at reasonable expense[8]
The council must hold a meeting with the landlord to discuss the future of the house. The landlord can give an undertaking either to go ahead and do the repairs anyway (although this rarely happens) or not to allow anyone to live there. If the landlord does not agree to either of these, then the council must take one of three courses of action:

- It can make a *demolition order* on the house requiring it to be knocked down.
- If a demolition order cannot be served (for example because the house is part of a terrace) then it must serve a *closing order* which makes it illegal for anyone to live there.
- As an alternative to a demolition or a closing order, the council can serve a *purchase notice*. The local authority can use this procedure to purchase the property if it believes it is suitable for use as temporary accommodation.

The right to rehousing and compensation if your home is closed or demolished
If the council decides to close or demolish your home, you lose your protection from eviction (see Chapter 2), but you have a right to rehousing by the local council and usually have a right to financial compensation as well (see page 21 for more details).

If your home is not unfit but is in need of repair
Local councils have powers to require landlords to do repairs even though the house is not unfit. If the property is in *substantial disrepair* the council can serve a notice on the landlord under Section 190 of the Housing Act 1985. If the repairs are not so substantial, but are still serious enough to interfere with your comfort, then a notice can also be served under Section 190. Both types of notice give details of the repairs needed and a time limit for doing the work. There is a minimum time limit of 21 days. If the work is not done within the time limit, the council then has the power to step in and do the work itself, claiming the cost from the landlord. However, councils do not have to do this, and are often reluctant to do so because of the time and expense

involved. If the council has served a notice but is failing to take further action get advice, as it may be possible to push the council to take it further. Even if the council does decide to take action it can take several months to organise this kind of work. The council can also prosecute the landlord, who can be fined.

ENFORCING YOUR RIGHTS TO REPAIR

If you are a private tenant you need to check whether or not you are a *regulated tenant* who has the full protection of the Rent Act 1977 or an assured tenant whose landlord is not able to use one of the grounds for possession in the Housing Act 1988 (see page 50). If you are not fully protected, any attempt to enforce your legal rights to repair could result in the landlord evicting you. If you think you may not be fully protected, get advice before taking any action.

The next step is to tell your landlord or the person who collects your rent what repairs need doing. If you do not know who your landlord is you have a legal right to be given the name and address by the landlord's agent or the person who collects the rent (see page 149). You may need proof that you have told your landlord what needs to be done, so it is important to put your request for repairs in writing and to keep a copy of the letter. Even if you made your first request by word of mouth you should still follow it up with a letter. If the landlord still does not do the repairs there are different ways you can choose to enforce your rights:

- you can ask the local council to inspect the property and take action requiring the landlord to do the repairs;

- you can take action yourself which may include taking the landlord to court to get the repairs done and also to claim damages.

Often you can pursue more than one line of action at the same time. For example, you could notify the local authority and pursue your own action at the same time.

You should not simply stop paying rent in an attempt to force the landlord to do repairs, because the landlord may then start court action to evict you for arrears. Although there are certain circumstances in which it is possible to get the work done yourself and to deduct the cost from the rent (see page 126), or to set the cost of repairs against any rent arrears, you should never do this without good legal advice and support, as it could result in you losing your home.

Getting the council to require your landlord to do repairs

The legal powers and duties of local councils to require landlords to do repairs are described above. If your landlord is failing to do repairs you should contact the council's environmental health department and ask for an officer to visit your home. It is best to telephone before 10.00 a.m. or after 4.00 p.m. as the officers are usually out visiting in between those times. The Environmental Health Officer should arrange a date for a visit. Try to get the name of the person who is dealing with your case as you may need to contact him or her again. If there are other tenants in the house tell them about the visit, as the Environmental Health Officer may want to see the rest of the house.

Before the visit, it is a good idea to make a list of all the repairs you want to complain about and to give it to the officer. Keep a copy for yourself. Get the name of the officer who calls and ask to be kept informed about what the landlord will be required to do and how long he or she will be given to do it. Ask for a copy of any notices the council sends to the landlord. Environmental health departments do not always use all the powers available to them and are sometimes very slow to act. If the council is not using all its powers, is failing in its duties or is taking a long time to act, there are a number of actions you can take:

- Your local councillor or a local advice or law centre may be able to contact the council on your behalf.

- If you believe your house is unfit (see page 120 for the legal definition of unfit) but you cannot get the council to take any action then you may be able to get a JP, who can be found in the local Magistrates' Court, to require the council to make a full inspection of and report on your home.[9] The JP may want to visit your home to inspect it. If he or she thinks it is unfit, a formal representation will be made to the local council. The council is then under a duty to make a full inspection and to decide whether or not it is unfit. If it decides that the property is unfit it must follow the procedure set out on page 120. Even if it decides it is not unfit, you can still ask it to serve notices to get repairs done as set out on page 121.

Taking action yourself against the landlord

You can take your landlord to court directly, without the help of the local council. If you are considering doing this, always get advice first as there is a range of different types of action you can take. You may be able to get someone from an advice or law centre to represent you free of charge, or you may get help under the Legal Aid Acheme (see page 166).

There are advantages and disadvantages to taking action yourself. The main advantages are:

- *Time:* If you can get an early court hearing this can be quicker than getting the council to serve notices. Many cases do not reach court because the landlord does the repairs before the hearing. But courts in some areas are very busy and delays can be quite long, especially if you have to wait for legal aid to be agreed first (see page 166).

- *Money:* In certain actions you can claim for damages to property or decorations and for inconvenience to yourself.

The main disadvantages are:

- *Costs:* You may have to pay solicitors' fees and court costs, although this rarely happens if you have a reasonable case. If you get help with the costs through legal aid, the cost of this may be taken out of any compensation you get.

- *Limitations:* You cannot be sure the court will grant you everything you ask for.

- *Proof:* You and your advisers will be responsible for providing proof of the problem and of how it is affecting you. This may mean getting a surveyor or Environmental Health Officer to provide an independent report. In addition, you may need to take photographs of the disrepair and prove damages to your belongings if you wish to claim compensation. You have a right to summon witnesses, for example the local council's Environmental Health Officer and to obtain relevant documents from the landlord.

If you decide to take action yourself your main rights are set out in:

- Section 11 of the Landlord and Tenant Act 1985
- Section 99 of the Public Health Act 1936
- The Defective Premises Act 1972
- Your tenancy agreement.

If your landlord fails to repair the structure or fixtures: Section 11, Landlord and Tenant 1985

Section 11 sets out the legal responsibilities of landlords to keep the structure and installations of the building repaired (see page 117). If your landlord fails to do this you can apply to the County Court for:

- an *order* that the work is done, **and**
- *damages* for the cost of any loss you have suffered and for your inconvenience.[10]

In order to take action you must first make sure that your landlord has been given reasonable notice that the repairs are needed. Put your request in writing and keep a copy. What is a reasonable time will depend on all the circumstances, including the scale of the work needed and the effect the disrepair is having on you. If your landlord does not do the work then it is advisable to get a solicitor or adviser to help and represent you. Many cases are settled before the court hearing, but you may have to go to court. The court will take into account a number of other factors:

- Can the repairs be done at *reasonable expense*?
- *The age, character, locality and potential lifespan of the building and the neighbourhood.* If you live in an old house in a run down area the court will not expect such a high standard of repair as for other areas or for more modern homes.

The court can decide whether or not to order the repairs to be done, but must, if the case is proved, award damages.

Getting repairs done: Section 99 Public Health Act 1936

Section 99 enables you to take the landlord to court yourself, if the disrepair counts as a *statutory nuisance* (see page 118 for the definition of this).

You should get advice before taking any action. Legal aid is not available for taking the case to court, although you may get advice before the hearing with the help of the legal aid Green Form Scheme (see page 166). If you decide to go ahead, then you or your legal representative take out a summons in the Magistrates' Court giving details of the problem. The summons will set a date for a court hearing where both sides can put their case. The magistrate may also want to visit your home. If the court decides there is a statutory nuisance then it **must:**

- order the landlord to end the nuisance by doing the repairs within a certain time. This is known as a 'nuisance order'.

It **may** also:

- fine the landlord, **and**
- grant you compensation (if you have asked for it), and costs.

If all the work is not done within the time ordered, you can go back to court for a further order, fines and compensation.

Other legal actions
In addition to these actions, if may be possible to:

- sue the landlord for damages equal to the difference between the value of your home in its repaired and unrepaired condition;
- get a court order for repairs which are specified as being the landlord's responsibility in the tenancy agreement;
- sue the landlord for damages for any negligence on his or her part.

You will need advice before taking any of these actions.

Defective Premises Act 1972
Under Section 4 of the Defective Premises Act 1972 a landlord who has an obligation to carry out repairs **or** who has a right to enter premises to carry out repairs, has a legal duty to prevent injury to people or damage to property arising from defects in the premises. This Act does not actually help directly in getting repairs done, but it does provide a way of getting compensation for personal injury or damage to property. The landlord's duty arises if he or she knows of the defect or should have known of it. So even if the landlord did not actually know of the disrepair but **should** have known, you might be able to sue him or her for compensation. These rights cover not only tenants, but also licensees and visitors of the tenant or licensee of the premises.

USING THE RENT TO PAY FOR THE REPAIRS

Many tenants faced with a landlord unwilling to do repairs, particularly minor repairs costing up to a few hundred pounds, and reluctant to get the council involved or to threaten legal action, decide to do the repairs themselves and deduct the cost of the repairs from the rent.

This course of action is risky, but the common law right of tenants to do the repairs themselves has been confirmed by the courts in recent years.

If you wish to use this self-help remedy, you should carefully follow the steps listed below.

○ Give notice in writing to your landlord of the repairs that need doing, keeping a copy of your letter (and all subsequent letters).

○ Obtain two or three estimates for the repairs from reputable builders.

○ After a reasonable time has elapsed, write again, enclosing copies of the estimates, stating that the landlord is in breach of his or her repairing obligations and that unless the work is done within a specified period (say two weeks) you will do the work yourself and deduct the cost from the rent.

○ If there is no response, go ahead with the work and when you pay your contractor make sure you obtain proper receipts.

○ Work out exactly how many weeks' rent you will be withholding. Only rent can be deducted. You have to continue paying any other sums you owe the landlord, such as service charges or rates.

○ Write to your landlord, explaining precisely how the rent deductions will be made to cover the cost of the work.

○ Withhold rent until the cost of the repairs has been covered.

You may be entitled to withhold an extra amount to cover, for example, damage done to your property, or the distress and inconvenience suffered. You should provide the landlord with the documentary evidence you have, ask for reimbursement, and state that if he or she fails to pay you, you will have to recover this sum by deducting it from your rent. It is best to claim too little rather than too much when asking for additional compensation. This is because if the court decide that you have withheld too much rent, they will order you to pay your landlord some back rent and you may be asked to pay your landlord's legal costs as well.

You should not run into arrears before doing the repairs, although, understandably enough, some tenants decide to stop payment as a means of trying to force the landlord to do the repairs.

If your landlord decides to sue you or to try to evict you for rent arrears, you can 'set-off' the total cost of the work (plus additional compensation you are claiming) in defending the action for rent arrears. You would need legal advice to do this.

Taking this self-help remedy requires careful preparation. If you are thinking of using it, get advice first.

GETTING IMPROVEMENTS DONE

If your home does not have one or more of the *standard amenities*, you may be able to get the local council to order your landlord to install them.[11] The standard amenities are:

- a fixed bath or shower;
- a wash hand basin;
- a sink;
- a hot and cold water supply to all the above;
- a toilet inside the dwelling.

The local council can serve a compulsory improvement notice on the landlord if your home was built or converted before 3 October 1961 and if it can be improved at reasonable expense. The council may require that it is brought up to the *full standard*, meaning the exclusive use of all the amenities, a reasonable state of repair, proper insulation, and that the dwelling is fit for human habitation and is likely to be available for the next 15 years. However, the local council may decide to impose only a *reduced standard*, meaning that not all these conditions have to be met.

If you live in a *Housing Action Area* or a *General Improvement Area* (see below), the council might decide to serve an improvement notice at any time. If you do not live in one of these areas the council can only take action if you ask it to do so in writing.

Once the council decides to take action it will serve a *provisional notice* on the landlord, the landlord's agent (if any) and on the tenant. The notice describes the work to be done and gives details of the time and place of a meeting to discuss the proposed improvements. You can attend this meeting and express your views. The local council can accept an undertaking from the landlord that the work will be done. If no such undertaking is given or accepted then the council may (but does not have to) serve a full *improvement notice* ordering the work to be done. If the improvement is to be to the *full standard* then the landlord must be given 12 months to complete the work, but a shorter time may be given if only a *reduced standard* is required. The landlord can appeal to the County Court against this notice, although in practice very few do so. The landlord can also serve a counter-notice on the local council, requiring it to purchase the property. If this happens the council must buy it and you will become a tenant of the council. If the landlord simply fails to carry out the work, the council can then do the work itself (although it does not have to do so) and claim the cost from the landlord.

If the council uses this compulsory improvement procedure, it must make sure that you have proper housing arrangements while the work is carried out.

This could mean either the landlord or the council providing you with temporary accommodation, with a guarantee that you can return to your home after the improvements. If you have to move permanently because an improvement notice has been served on your home, you have rights to rehousing and to compensation from the council (see page 21). This procedure for compulsory improvement takes a long time and can be very expensive for the council. For this reason it is only rarely used.

Housing action areas and general improvement areas
These are special areas that can be declared by local councils. Councils tell local residents when they are declaring an area and you will probably know if you live in one. If you are not sure you can always check at the council offices. In these areas councils have greater powers to improve properties and to purchase them. There are also more generous improvement grants available (see page 138).

Doing improvements yourself
If you are a fully protected tenant and you haven't been given notice by your landlord that one of the mandatory Rent Act grounds for possession applies (see page 60), you have the same rights as public sector tenants to do improvements (see page 151) and to apply for grants (see page 138) to help with the cost. You have to get the written agreement of your landlord, but this cannot be unreasonably withheld. If you spend your own money on improvements you do not have a right to claim it back from the landlord even if you paid for work which the landlord could have been made to do. On the other hand, the landlord cannot normally put up the rent because of improvements you have done.

OVERCROWDING

The law on overcrowding affects both landlords and tenants.[12] There are two different tests of overcrowding. If you fail **either** of these tests then you are *statutorily overcrowded*.

- *The Room Standard:* By this test you are overcrowded if there are so many people in your home that two or more people aged over 10 of opposite sexes are forced to sleep in the same room. Couples living together as man and wife do not count; nor do children under 10. All rooms have to be taken into account, not just bedrooms. The living room and even the kitchen may be counted if it is big enough to hold a bed.

- *The Space Standard:* The second test gives the maximum number of people who may live in accommodation of a particular size. There are two different ways of assessing this. You have to work out both ways and then take whichever is the lower number of people as the maximum number who are allowed to live there.

First, take the number of people living there: children between one and 10 years old count as half a person and children under a year old do not count at all. Next, count up the number of living rooms. A kitchen can count as a living room, but rooms of less than 50 square feet do not count. The following table shows the maximum number of people allowed for each number of rooms:

Number of rooms	Number of people allowed
1	2
2	3
3	5
4	7½
5	10
Each extra room	2 extra people

The other test is based on the size of rooms and shows the number of people (calculated in the same way as before) allowed in each room size. The following table shows the number of people allowed in each size of room:

Size of room	Number of people allowed
Less than 50 square feet	0
50-69 square feet	½
70-89 square feet	1
90-109 square feet	1½
110 square feet and more	2

If you fail **either** of these *space standard* tests or if you fail the *room standard* test then you are, in law, overcrowded and you and the landlord may be committing an offence and may be prosecuted by the local council. However, in certain circumstances, overcrowding may be permitted. First, the tenant (but not the landlord) can apply to the local council for a licence for not more than a year at a time to allow overcrowding. Second, if the overcrowding is caused by members of your family staying with you temporarily this does not count as illegal overcrowding. Third, the overcrowding may have occurred by *natural growth*, in other words a child reaches the age where it counts as an extra half or one person, thereby taking the family over the permitted number of people. If this occurs and you apply to the local council for alternative accommodation before any prosecution, then the overcrowding is not considered illegal. If, however, the local council offers you suitable alternative accommodation and you turn it down, the overcrowding will be illegal.

If you are illegally overcrowded the landlord can go to court to evict you.

HOUSES IN MULTIPLE OCCUPATION

Local councils have extra powers they can use in houses in multiple occupation (HMOs). An HMO is a house which is occupied by more than one separate household.[13] Examples of HMOs include:

- houses split into bedsits;
- hostels;
- houses where one family lives upstairs and another downstairs;
- hotels housing homeless people.

Councils have powers to make sure there are adequate facilities (for example baths and wash basins) provided in HMOs, that there are proper means of escape from fire and that there is no overcrowding. Councils can also take control of HMOs if they are not being properly managed.

Facilities

Each council has its own rules about the number of amenities such as wash basins, baths or cooking facilities which must be provided in HMOs. These rules are set out in the council's Code of Practice for Houses in Multiple Occupation. You can get a copy from the environmental health department of your local council. Normally each flat or room should have its own wash hand basin with hot and cold water, and reasonable access to cooking facilities (including an oven), either a refrigerator or a ventilated food cupboard and a means of heating. There will also be rules on the number of people who are allowed to share each bath or shower and toilet.

If you believe there are inadequate facilities in your home you should complain to the environmental health department. It is a good idea to tell the other tenants in the house, as the Environmental Health Officer may want to inspect the whole house; indeed you should ask him or her to do so.

The council may serve a notice on the landlord (or on the landlord's agent) ordering that any necessary extra facilities are installed and giving a time limit for the work to be completed.[14] If the work is not done the landlord can be prosecuted and the council can do the work itself and claim the cost from the landlord.[15] However, it is not obliged to do this.

Overcrowding in HMOs

The council may also serve notices if it regards the HMO as overcrowded.[16]

Councils have wider discretion in HMOs than in other housing to decide what is overcrowding and are not limited to the definitions of illegal overcrowding that apply to other properties (see page 129). Most commonly they will issue a *direction order* to reduce overcrowding, which means that the landlord cannot let to more people than the number specified on the order. If there are already more people living in the house no one is forced to leave but, when someone does go, the landlord is not allowed to relet until the number in the house has fallen below the number set by the order. If there are too many people in relation to the facilities available, the council can do one of three things:

- order the installation of more facilities;
- order that no more than a certain number of people live in the house;
- issue both types of notice, specifying the number of facilities that have to be provided and the maximum number of people who may live there.

Means of escape from fire

There is a greater risk of fires in HMOs, both because of their poor conditions and because of the number of people living in them. The local council can (and in some cases must) serve a notice on the landlord ordering works to ensure there are adequate means of escape from fire.[17] This can include an order preventing the landlord from letting out certain parts of the house. If this happens, any tenants who have to move have a right to rehousing and to compensation from the council (see page 21). If the works required are not done, the landlord may be prosecuted and the council can do the work itself and charge the cost to the landlord. For smaller HMOs these powers are discretionary — the local council does not have to use them. However, for larger buildings (houses of at least three storeys with a total floor area of over 500 square metres) local councils are obliged by law to use these powers.[18]

Management and control of HMOs

A landlord of an HMO should keep the house in good order. This includes repair and maintenance of the individual rooms, common parts such as hallway and stairs, and of the plumbing, drains, electrical wiring and gas supply and shared cookers and water heaters. If the landlord is seriously failing in these duties the council can serve a *management order* on the property.[19] This sets out the landlord's duties and the work necessary to bring the house up to standard. If the landlord fails to comply with the order, he or she can be prosecuted and the council can do the work itself, claiming the cost from the landlord.

If the council considers that the tenants' safety, welfare or health is in danger, it can impose a *control order* on the landlord.[20] This means that the council itself takes over the management of the house. However, control orders are very rarely used by councils.

Councils' use of their powers

Although councils have a wide range of powers to enforce repairs and improvements, with extra powers in HMOs, they are very often reluctant to use them. The more time-consuming and expensive the law is to enforce, the less likely are councils to do so. Even if they serve large numbers of notices under the Housing and Public Health Acts, they may fail to follow them up. Extensive powers such as control orders on HMOs are used very rarely indeed. If you are having difficulties in getting the council to use its legal powers, get advice.

HOUSING ASSOCIATION TENANTS: ACTION THROUGH A TENANTS' ASSOCIATION

Housing association tenants have all the same rights as tenants of private landlords to get repairs done but, because their landlords are publicly accountable and non-profit-making, they may be able to make swifter progress in getting repairs done by putting pressure on the landlord through a tenants' association.

HOUSING ASSOCIATION TENANTS: A NEW 'RIGHT TO REPAIR'

Housing association tenants now have a right to carry out repairs themselves and to receive payment from their landlord. The scheme is the same as that for council tenants (see page 136).

Council tenants

Council tenants have many of the same legal rights to repair as private tenants. However, there are two big differences. First, local councils cannot serve notices on themselves requiring work to be done, so council tenants cannot make use of the legal provisions which require the service of notices by Environmental Health Officers. However, councils have been encouraged by a Government Circular[21] to introduce and publish arrangements whereby, if a council tenant calls in an Environmental Health Officer, the officer will notify the housing department of any defects which would in the private sector lead to notices being served under the Housing Act 1985 (see page 120). The housing department should then ensure that the necessary repairs are carried out within a reasonable time.

The second main difference between council and private tenants is that councils are democratically elected and publicly accountable. This means that it may be more effective to put public pressure on the council to do repairs than to take legal action.

Councils, like private landlords, have legal responsibility for the structure and fixtures of the building under Section 11 of the Landlord and Tenant Act 1985 (see page 117 for more details of the items for which they are responsible). Councils are responsible for those items even if the tenancy agreement says that they are not. The only circumstance in which these items may not be the responsibility of the landlord is where the tenant has claimed a *right to repair* under the Housing Act 1985 (see page 136).

Responsibility for other items of repair will depend on what is set out in your tenancy agreement and the council should by law provide you with clear details of your rights to get repairs done.

If the repair is the council's responsibility you should inform it as soon as possible in writing. It is important to keep a copy of the letter as you may need evidence later on if there is any delay. You need to give the council reasonable time to do the repair. Some councils give guidelines to tenants on how long it will take to do particular jobs. Obviously some are more urgent than others. A broken sash cord may wait several weeks, but a toilet which is blocked and cannot be used should be repaired within 48 hours. Most councils have an emergency service for problems like this and if the repair is urgent you should ring the council directly.

If the repair is unreasonably delayed, contact the housing department again, confirming any telephone calls in writing. If you are still getting nowhere, then there are a number of things you can do to make the council do the repairs. You can:

- put extra pressure on the council, for example through your tenants' association or by contacting a local councillor;
- take the council to court to force it to do repairs and perhaps pay you compensation;
- in certain limited circumstances get the work done yourself and deduct the cost from the rent or claim reimbursement from the landlord.

You should never simply stop paying rent, as the council might then evict you for rent arrears, nor should you give up the tenancy. If you do either, you may find yourself homeless and the council may refuse you any further help (see page 17 on intentional homelessness). If you are in this position get advice immediately.

The best course of action will depend on your own circumstances. You can, of course, take legal action and put public pressure on the council at the same time. We now look in turn at the different courses of action.

PUTTING EXTRA PRESSURE ON THE COUNCIL

Unlike private landlords, councils are publicly accountable through their elected councillors. This means that putting public pressure on the council may be a more effective method of getting repairs done than legal action. The first step is to contact your tenants' association to ask them if they can take up your complaint. If there is no tenants' association you might consider getting together with other tenants to set one up. Tenants' associations can develop links with councillors and housing staff and can mount campaigns, so they can be more effective in taking up complaints than individuals, who can often be too easily ignored. Action through tenants' associations may be particularly important if the problem is one that affects a group of tenants, for example building faults in an estate.

You can also take up the complaint directly with your local councillor. They are elected to represent you and good councillors will always be willing to take up individual complaints. You can find out the names of the local councillors for your neighbourhood from the Town Hall or local council office. Many hold local advice sessions (or surgeries) when you can call and see them. The Town Hall will have details of these sessions. Ask your local councillor to take up the complaint on your behalf. This can often be enough to get action from the housing department.

In addition, you could try getting a story in your local paper about the problem. No council likes bad publicity and local newspapers are always on the look out for stories. Telephone your local paper and ask for the News Desk. If you have a tenants' association ask for their help in getting publicity.

If all else fails, you could complain to the Local Government Ombudsman. The Ombudsman investigates cases of management inefficiency and unreasonable delay by local councils. They publish a booklet which explains how to complain, entitled *Your Local Ombudsman.* You can get a copy from advice centres or directly from the Ombudsman (see *Useful addresses*). The main drawbacks with the Ombudsman are that they often take many months to investigate and reach a decision and that they cannot order a council to do anything, although councils will usually take their findings very seriously.

TAKING ACTION YOURSELF

Environmental Health Officers cannot take their own councils to court. However, all those courses of action which can be taken directly by private tenants can also be taken by council tenants. These actions are:

- court action where the council has failed in its repairing obligations under Section 11 of the Housing Act 1985 (see page 117);
- court action under Section 99 of the Public Health Act 1936 (see page 125);
- making a complaint to a JP (see page 123);
- other actions for damages and to secure repairs which are the landlord's responsibility under the tenancy agreement (see page 126);
- using the rent to pay for repairs (see page 126).

If you are considering taking action always get independent advice first.

DOING MINOR REPAIRS YOURSELF

Council tenants and housing association tenants have a right to do minor repairs themselves.[22] Tenants who wish to do minor repairs themselves can serve a notice on the landlord stating their wish to do this. The landlord can refuse only on a limited number of grounds, for example because the work proposed by the tenant is unsatisfactory or because the landlord has firm plans to do the work. The scheme has a number of very serious drawbacks for tenants:

- Once the tenant takes up this right the landlord's legal obligations to carry out that particular repair are suspended.
- The tenant will be liable for damages if anything goes wrong. So, for example, if plumbing work is faulty and a leak floods the flat below the tenant could be liable for thousands of pounds worth of damages.
- The landlord may only meet a part of the cost of the work or even pay nothing at all if the work goes wrong, leaving the tenant out of pocket.

You should get advice before deciding to exercise this right rather than one of the other legal rights to repair.

HOUSING ACTION TRUSTS

The Housing Act 1988 creates a new form of landlord called a Housing Action Trust. They will take over areas of run down housing, normally from local councils, and aim to repair and improve the homes in the area as well as improving the general environment. When the improvements have been completed, the properties will be passed on to other landlords, who may be housing associations or private landlords or possibly back to the council. Tenants in the area should be consulted about the setting up of the Trust and about its plans, and will be able to vote on whether they want to be taken over by the Trust.

The Trusts will take over many of the powers of the local authority, including the provision of homes and powers under the Housing and Public Health Acts to deal with bad housing conditions. Tenants will have most of the same rights as council tenants while their landlord is the Trust, but they will not necessarily keep these rights if they subsequently transfer to a private landlord. They are also likely to have to pay higher rents.

There will at first be only a handful of Housing Action Trusts in the country and you should hear if there are any proposals for your area.

PEOPLE IN COUNCIL TEMPORARY ACCOMMODATION

The position of people in council temporary accommodation is more complicated than that of permanent council tenants. The most important thing is to know whether you are classed as a *tenant* or a *licensee*, as this will affect your rights.

Tenant or licensee?

Most councils do not accept people in their hostels or reception centres or other temporary accommodation owned by them as tenants, but merely as licensees, who have fewer rights to repairs. To find out if you are a tenant or a licensee, you should look at your rent book or other papers which the council gave you when you moved in. These will include either the words 'licensee' and 'licence agreement' or the words 'tenant' and 'tenancy agreement'.

If you are a *tenant* in temporary accommodation, you have almost the same rights as permanent tenants. However, in some cases the council is allowed to use *unfit* properties (see page 120 for the definition of unfit) on a temporary basis. This is usually where the council bought the property from a private owner because it was unfit, but it is considered adequate for use until it can be repaired or demolished. In these circumstances you cannot make a complaint to a JP (see page 123).

If you are a *licensee* you have fewer rights. Section 11 of the Landlord and Tenant Act 1985 (see page 117) does not apply to you, so the council's responsibility for repairs is not clearly laid down. You can however use Section 99 of the Public Health Act 1936 (see page 125) and can sue for damages (see page 126).

If you have been put in a *privately-owned* bed and breakfast hotel or hostel by the council you are not a council tenant or licensee. You do still, however, have legal rights which will depend on the type of letting you have. Get advice.

Improvement, repairs and insulation grants for home owners, tenants and landlords

There are special grants available from local councils to help with the cost of improving run down homes.[23] These grants are for bringing houses up to a decent standard — for example, installing an inside toilet or doing major roof repairs. Often, however, many of these discretionary grants are not available because the local council's allocation of money has run out. They are not available for work such as building an extension to your home.

They can be claimed by home owners, landlords and tenants. You cannot normally get a grant for work you have already started and should also check with the local council whether planning permission is required and what building regulations may apply before starting work.

TYPES OF GRANT

There are four main types of grant:

- *Improvement grants* are for major improvements, or for converting a house into flats, along with any necessary repairs. These grants are discretionary — the council can decide whether or not to give you one.

- *Intermediate grants* are for installing basic amenities (an inside toilet, bath, sink, wash basin and hot and cold water) along with any necessary repairs. These grants are mandatory — the council must give you an intermediate grant if you qualify for one.

- *Repairs grants* are for houses built before 1919 where substantial and structural repairs are necessary. They are normally discretionary — the council can decide whether or not to give you one. But if the council has served a notice on you ordering you to do the repairs under Section 190 of the Housing Act 1985 (see page 120) then it must give you one as long as you meet the other conditions for a grant (see below).

- *Special grants* are for landlords only and are for installing basic amenities and means of escape from fire in houses in multiple occupation and for any necessary repairs. They are normally discretionary; the council can decide whether or not to give you one. But if the council has served notices ordering you to do the work under Section 352 of the Housing Act 1985 or Sections 365 to 368 of the Housing Act 1985 for work in an HMO it must give you a grant (see page 131).

WHO CAN CLAIM A GRANT

If you are a *home owner* you must fulfil **all** the following conditions to claim a grant:

- you are a freeholder, or have a lease with at least five years to run, **and**
- the work is being done on your only or main home for you or members of your family, **and**
- your home is within the age limits set out on page 140, **and**
- the rateable value of your home is not more than £400 in Greater London or £225 elsewhere. If, however, you are claiming an improvement grant to convert a house into separate flats, one of them for yourself, the rateable value limits are £600 in Greater London or £350 elsewhere. There are no rateable value limits at all if you are applying for an intermediate grant to install basic amenities in a house in a Housing Action Area. If you are claiming an *improvement* or *intermediate grant* to do work to make your home suitable for a person with a disability, then there are no rateable value limits on the house.

If you are a *landlord* you must fulfil **all** of the following conditions to claim a grant:

- you are a freeholder or have a lease with at least five years to run, **and**
- you will continue to let the property to tenants who are not members of the landlord's family and it must be rented by them as their main home, not, for example, as a holiday home, **and**
- the property is within the age limits set out below.

The following *tenants* can apply for a grant:

- Regulated private tenants (see page 52).
- Secure tenants of public landlords (see page 79).
- Long leaseholders on low rents with less than five years left on the lease.
- Protected occupiers and statutory tenants under the Rent (Agriculture) Act 1976 (see page 64).

The property must be within the age limits set out below.

Age limits of properties

If you are claiming an *improvement* or an *intermediate grant* the property must have been built or converted before 1961. However, this limit does not apply if you are claiming one of these grants to make the property suitable for a disabled person.

If you are claiming a *repairs grant*, the property must have been built before 1919.

HOW MUCH IS THE GRANT?

To work out how much grant you can get the council will first take the cost of the work you want to do. There are maximum limits, however, which councils cannot exceed, known as the *eligible expense* limits. The council cannot take account of any costs above the eligible expense. These limits are set out in Table 1.

Table 1

	In Greater London	Elsewhere
Improvement grants:		
Priority cases:	£16,900	£12,600
(Unfit properties Properties in Housing Action Areas. Improvement of properties for disabled people.)		
Other, non-priority cases.	£11,000	£8,100
Intermediate grants:		
Installing amenities	£3,940	£3,010
Repairs	£4,850	£3,450
Repair grants:	£7,600	£5,500

Special grants:		
Amenities (for each):		
Fixed bath or shower	£590	£450
Wash hand basin	£230	£170
Sink	£590	£450
Hot and cold water supply to:		
Fixed bath or shower	£750	£570
Wash hand basin	£390	£305
Sink	£500	£385
WC	£890	£680
Fire escape works	£12,420	£9,315
Repairs works	£4,850	£3,450

Having calculated the cost of the works (up to the maximum allowed by the eligible expense limits) the council will then work out what *proportion* of the cost will be met by the grant. The proportions of the cost met by the grant are:

Special grants	20 per cent
Priority cases (see table above)	75 per cent
Properties in General Improvement Areas	65 per cent
All other cases	50 per cent

If you are converting a house into flats and intend to live in one of the flats yourself there are higher eligible expense limits. These are for each flat provided.

Table 2

	In Greater London	Elsewhere
Houses of 3 or more storeys:		
Priority cases (see above, Table 1)	£19,600	£14,500
Non-priority cases	£12,700	£9,400
Other conversions:		
Priority cases (see above, Table 1)	£16,900	£12,500
Non-priority cases	£11,000	£8,100

There are special higher limits for buildings listed as being of special architectural or historical interest.

If the council decides you could not pay your share of the cost without undue hardship, it may give a higher grant of up to 90 per cent in priority cases or when giving a special grant or up to 65 per cent in other cases.

To show how the calculation works, suppose you live outside London and want to do improvements at a cost of £8,000 but are not a priority case. You apply for an ordinary *improvement grant.*

Cost of work	£10,000
Eligible expense limit for non-priority case outside London	£8,100
Proportion of eligible expense for non-priority	50 per cent
GRANT	£4,050

To show how the calculation works, suppose you live outside London and want to do improvements at a cost of £8,000 but are not a priority case. You apply for an ordinary *improvement grant.*

AFTER THE IMPROVEMENT WORK

There are rules to prevent owners of property using improvement grants for second homes or for financial gain. If you are a home owner, you have to sign a certificate that you or close relatives intend to live in the house for five years. You are allowed to sell to another owner occupier or after one year to let it to tenants, but if it is used in any other way (for example, as a second home) the council may require the grant to be repaid with interest.

If you are a landlord you will have to sign a certificate stating that you intend to let the property as a home (not to a member of your family) for five years; other conditions on the type of letting may also be added. If the property is used in any other way, for example sold to an owner occupier or let for holiday purposes, the council may require the grant to be repaid with interest.

INSULATION GRANTS

In addition to improvement grants, some people can also claim an insulation grant from the local council towards the cost of insulating lofts, hot water tanks and pipes.[24] You qualify for a grant if you are getting Family Credit or Income Support from the DSS or Housing Benefit from the local authority.

Home owners, tenants and landlords can apply for a grant of 90 per cent of the cost of the work or £137, whichever is the lower amount. You can get details from your local council.

5: Other rights of tenants and long leaseholders

In addition to protection from eviction and rights over repairs and rents, tenants have a variety of other rights. This chapter describes those rights.

Private tenants

HARASSMENT AND ILLEGAL EVICTION

Some landlords, if they cannot evict their tenants legally, will try to get them out by making life difficult, perhaps by withdrawing services such as gas and electricity or by threatened or actual violence. This is known as *harassment*. If the landlord actually throws you out before he or she is entitled to, or changes the locks while you are out, this is known as *illegal eviction*. Most tenants and licensees are protected from both harassment and illegal eviction.[1] You can also sue for damages and for an order allowing you to get back in.

Harassment: Who is protected

The law against harassment protects all *residential occupiers*. This covers the vast majority of people living in rented accommodation, including:

- All tenants and ex-tenants continuing to live in the property after the tenancy has ended.
- Licensees who have not been given reasonable notice by their landlord.
- Licensees who have restricted contracts (see page 76) entered into on or after 28 November 1980, even if the licence has been brought to an end by the landlord.
- Service occupiers with exclusive possession (see page 63), even after their contract of employment has ended.
- Rental purchasers.[2]

The main categories of people not covered by the law against harassment are:

- Licensees who do not come into one of the categories listed above, **and**
- Squatters.

However, even in these cases the landlord may well commit an offence under other laws if any violence is used or threatened in the eviction, or if entry is forced into your home while you are in it.

Illegal Eviction: Who is protected

If your tenancy or licence began before 15 January 1989 and you are a residential occupier (see above) then you are protected by the law against illegal eviction. However, if your tenancy or licence began on or after January 1989, or you have agreed a rent increase other than one set by a Rent Officer or Rent Tribunal, and you come into one of the following categories, then you will not be protected by the law against illegal eviction. Those who are excluded from protection are:

- People who share living accommodation with the landlord or landlord's family.
- People who were originally squatters and who have been given a temporary tenancy or licence of the property.
- People in a holiday letting.
- Licensees in a hostel provided by a local council, a housing association or some other public bodies.
- People living in rent-free accommodation.

All other tenants and licensees remain protected from illegal eviction, regardless of when their tenancy or licence began.

What to do

If you suffer from harassment or illegal eviction, contact the tenancy relations officer who is employed by the local council. The tenancy relations officer will normally try first to conciliate between you and your landlord, explaining the law to the landlord and that he or she is not allowed to harass you or to evict you without going to court. If this is unsuccessful, the tenancy relations officer may then decide to prosecute the landlord. Unfortunately however, courts often impose only very small fines on landlords and these do not deter the really unscrupulous ones. The court can also award compensation to you for personal injury, loss or damage.

In addition to action by the tenancy relations officer, you can yourself take action through the civil courts. Get advice before doing this; if you have a local law centre they are often best able to help on this sort of case. You or your adviser will be able to apply, usually to the County Court, for an *injunction.* This is an order telling the landlord to stop harassing you and, if you have been illegally evicted, to let you back into your home. If the landlord disobeys this, he or she can be fined or sent to prison. If the case is urgent you can go to the court for a temporary emergency order without the landlord being able to put his or her case. This is known as an *ex parte* injunction; it normally lasts only for a short period of up to a week, after which there will be another hearing with both parties present. At that hearing another order may be made, pending the full hearing of the case at which, if necessary, a final injunction will be granted. Along with the injunction you can also ask for damages which could amount to several thousand pounds in certain circumstances.

Remember that good legal advice should always be sought. Legal aid is available for these actions (see page 166).

WHEN A TENANT'S FAMILY CAN INHERIT THE TENANCY

If a tenancy is in joint names and one of the tenants dies, the other is automatically entitled to stay on as a tenant. When a fully protected *regulated tenant* (see page 52) dies and the tenancy was in that person's name only, the tenancy passes automatically to the husband or wife of the deceased tenant.[3] The surviving member of a couple who were living together but not married can inherit the tenancy in this way. If there is no spouse, then it passes to any member of the family who had been living in the home for at least two years prior to the tenant's death. However, that person will only have an assured tenancy (see page 67 for what this means). When an *assured tenant* dies the tenancy passes to their spouse or the surviving member of a couple who were living together. This right to inherit the tenancy is known as *succeeding* to the tenancy and in all the cases mentioned above there is the right to only one such succession. So the original tenant can be followed by one further tenant who succeeds to the tenancy.

THE RIGHT TO A RENT BOOK AND RECEIPTS FOR RENT

If you have a weekly tenancy and you are not provided with substantial board (see page 53), you have a legal right to a rent book from the landlord.[4] But no other tenants or licensees have this right. The tenancy relations officer of the local council can prosecute if the landlord refuses to provide a rent book to a tenant who is entitled to one. The rent book must contain information on the name and address of the landlord and agent (if any), on the rent payable, on your rights to have a rent fixed, on your protection from eviction and right to claim a rent allowance.

If you are not entitled to a rent book from your landlord, try to get receipts or at least pay by cheque, so that the payment is recorded. This is important in case the landlord later tries to claim that you have not paid the rent. If the landlord will only take cash and refuses to give receipts, try to pay in the presence of a witness. Write to the landlord to request a receipt and keep a copy of the letter.

WHEN THE LANDLORD CAN ENTER YOUR HOME

Landlords have the right to enter occasionally to inspect the property for any repairs which it is their obligation to carry out. However, he or she should give you at least 24 hours' notice and arrange a reasonable time of day.[5] If the landlord is persistently entering without your permission, he or she may be trespassing and you may be able to take legal action to prevent it.

IF YOU DO NOT WANT YOUR LANDLORD TO DO IMPROVEMENTS

If your landlord is planning to make improvements to your home and you do not want them done, you may be able to prevent them if you are a fully protected tenant (see page 52). The landlord can only do improvements against your wishes if:

- your tenancy agreement states that he or she can do so; **or**
- the landlord has applied for an improvement grant from the local council, it is likely to be approved **and** he or she has been to court to get permission to carry out the improvements against your wishes. You can dispute the landlord's plans in court and in reaching a decision the judge will take into account your age and health, what accommodation arrangements will be made for you while the work is carried out and the inconvenience to you[6]; **or**
- the landlord is legally obliged to carry out the work.

If you have to move out during the building work make sure that your right to return to the property is agreed in writing by the landlord.

Get advice before agreeing to any proposals by the landlord or before deciding to dispute them.

A LIST OF FURNITURE

If the tenancy is *furnished* you should arrange to agree with the landlord a list of the furniture provided. This is known as an *inventory*. It should include a note on the condition of each item. This should help to prevent future disputes about any damage to the furniture. Normally, the landlord does not have to provide an inventory by law, unless you paid a lump sum for the furniture at the beginning of the tenancy.[7] If the landlord refuses to supply one, you could make your own and send a copy, asking him or her to tell you if there are any inaccuracies.

NO CHILDREN ALLOWED

Many landlords say that no children are allowed. If this is part of your tenancy agreement and you have children, or bring them to live with you, then you will be breaking your tenancy agreement. However, if the landlord goes to court to evict you and you are a fully protected or assured tenant, you could claim that it is *not reasonable* to evict you for this reason (see page 57 for protected tenants and page 70 for assured tenants). If the landlord made no mention of children not being allowed at the beginning of the tenancy, he or she cannot later use it as a ground for trying to evict you.

If, however, you bring children into the accommodation and thereby cause illegal overcrowding, you might be evicted on these grounds (see page 129 for more details of overcrowding and the circumstances in which it is permitted).

CHANGING THE TENANCY AGREEMENT

There is nothing to stop the landlord and tenant agreeing to change the terms of the tenancy at any time. But the key word here is *agreement*. Both sides must agree any change and one side cannot impose a change on the other. If the landlord does ask you to sign a new agreement at any time after you have moved in, get advice before signing anything because you could be reducing your legal rights by entering into a new agreement. You do not have to sign anything and, if you do not, the terms of the old agreement will continue to apply.

If you are a regulated tenant and you sign an agreement to pay a higher rent, this does not prevent you from later applying to the Rent Officer for a fair rent to be fixed (see page 91). The agreement to increase the rent must be in writing and must state at the top that you do not have to sign the agreement, that your security will not be affected if you do not and that you can apply to the Rent Officer for a fair rent to be fixed at any time.[8]

FUEL COSTS: WHAT LANDLORDS CAN CHARGE

If you pay your landlord for the use of gas and electricity there is a maximum amount that he or she can charge for each unit of fuel you use. Gas and electricity boards in each area of the country publish these tariffs and you should get a copy from them if you suspect you might be overcharged. Get advice, as you can recover any excess.

For a detailed guide to fuel problems see *The Fuel Rights Handbook* published by SHAC.

Private tenants and long leaseholders

BUYING THE FREEHOLD OF THE BUILDING FROM THE LANDLORD

Private tenants and long leaseholders have a right of first refusal if their landlord wants to sell the freehold of their building. This right does not apply, however, to assured tenants (see page 67), tenants of resident landlords or service tenants (see page 63).[9] To qualify as resident for this purpose the landlord must have lived in a flat in the building as his or her only or main home for at least a year before selling the freehold. However, the landlord does not count as resident if the building was originally built as a block of flats.

If the landlord sells the property without first offering it to the tenants and long leaseholders then they can require the new owner to sell it to them for the same price.

You may also be able to force the landlord to sell to you if the landlord has persistently failed to manage the building properly and is likely to continue doing so and the appointment of a manager (see below) would be unlikely to solve the problem.

You should get together with the other occupants of the building and get legal advice if you want to buy from the landlord under one of these procedures.

APPOINTMENT OF A MANGER FOR THE PROPERTY

If the landlord has failed to manage the property properly, including failure to do repairs, then tenants and long leaseholders can apply to the court to appoint a manager to carry out these duties.[10] This right does not apply to assured tenants (see page 67) or tenants of resident landlords.

CHANGING THE LEASE

Owners of leasehold properties whose lease is longer than 21 years can apply to the court to change the lease if it does not contain satisfactory arrangements for repairs, insurance, or services.[11] Get legal advice if you believe your lease is inadequate.

THE RIGHT TO KNOW THE NAME OF THE LANDLORD

You have a legal right to know the name of your landlord. If you cannot find out the landlord's name write to the person who last collected rent from you stating that you are requesting a written statement of the landlord's full name and address and pointing out that you have a right to this information under Part IV of the Landlord and Tenant Act 1987. Send the letter by recorded delivery so they cannot deny having received it, and keep copies of all correspondence. If the landlord's agent fails to respond to this the tenancy relations officer (see page 144) can prosecute them and you may be able to withhold rent or service charges under certain circumstances, but get advice before doing so. You can also get details of your landlord from your local Land Registry; look for the address in the telephone directory. For further details of the rights of long leaseholders see: *Owning your flat* published by SHAC.

Council and housing association tenants

Most council and other public sector tenants (see page 80 for a full list) are secure tenants and have a range of additional rights under the Housing Act 1985. Housing association tenants whose tenancy began before 15 January 1989 are usually also secure tenants and have the same legal rights as council tenants. Those whose tenancy began on or after that date are usually assured tenants (see page 67). They do not have the same rights set down in law but most of the rights described in this section should be spelt out for them in their tenancy agreement.

THE RIGHT TO INHERIT THE TENANCY

If the tenancy is in joint names and one of the tenants dies, the other automatically stays on as tenant. If the tenancy is in one person's name and that person dies, it passes to their husband or wife (if they have been living together) or to another member of the *family* who has been living with the tenant for at least a year before the tenant died.[12] This is known as the *right to succeed to the tenancy*. The definition of *family* is very wide,[13] so the right to succeed to the tenancy applies to all of the following: husband, wife, parent, grandparent, child, grandchild, brother, sister, uncle, aunt, nephew, niece, stepchild, illegitimate child, and couples living together as man and wife but not married. Relationships by marriage and half relationships also count.

These rights to succeed to the tenancy only apply to one succession, and if the tenancy passed from joint tenants to one of the tenants this too counts as a succession. After one succession it is up to the landlord whether you can stay or not. So, for example, if a man had the tenancy in his name and died, his wife would have the right to succeed, but when she died any remaining family members would not have that right, although the landlord may agree to let them stay on. If you are the wife or husband of the deceased tenant and you succeed to the tenancy, the landlord cannot then try to move you to smaller accommodation. If, however, you are another member of the family, or you were not married to your partner, and you succeed to the tenancy, the landlord can ask the court for permission to move you to suitable alternative accommodation, but **only** if they can prove that your present home is larger than you reasonably need **and** if they give you written notice of their intention to do this between six and 12 months after the present tenant's death (see page 84 for more details).

THE RIGHT TO TAKE IN LODGERS AND TENANTS

If you want to rent out part of your home, different rules apply depending on whether you let it to a *lodger* or to a *tenant*.[14] The legal difference is that a lodger is only a licensee. The difference depends on the degree of control you keep over rooms which are let out. If you share living accommodation and eat together the person is almost certainly a lodger. If you let a self-contained part of your home, do not share any rooms with the person you let to and do not provide them with any food or services such as cleaning, that person will probably be a tenant (see page 51 for more details on the differences between licensees and tenants).

You have the right to take in *lodgers* without getting your landlord's permission. You also have the right to let a part of your home (but not all of it) to a *tenant*, but must first get your landlord's written permission. The landlord cannot refuse permission without giving good reasons in writing. If they do refuse permission you can challenge this in the County Court. It is up to the landlord to prove they are being reasonable. They might, for example, argue that it would lead to overcrowding of the property. If you do decide to take in a lodger or tenant, both they and you will have certain legal rights and obligations and you should make sure you understand these before going ahead. See Chapter 2 for further details.

PASSING ON THE TENANCY TO SOMEONE ELSE

You are not normally allowed to pass the tenancy on to someone else.[15] The only exceptions to this are:

- when you exercise your right to exchange tenancies (see page 24);
- when property is transferred by the court to one partner after a divorce;
- when the person to whom you pass the tenancy is a member of your family who would have the right to succeed to the tenancy after your death and your landlord agrees to the tenancy being passed on. An attempt to pass on the tenancy without the landlord's agreement could lead to eviction of the new 'tenant'. However, if you do pass on the tenancy in this way, no one else will then have a right to succeed to the tenancy after that person's death (see page 149 on the *Right to inherit the tenancy).* The law in this area is complicated and you should get legal advice if you are thinking of passing on your tenancy in this way.

You can only pass on the tenancy (which is known as *assigning* the tenancy) in one of these three circumstances.

THE RIGHT TO EXCHANGE WITH ANOTHER TENANT

See page 24 for details.

THE RIGHT TO MAKE IMPROVEMENTS TO YOUR HOME

You have the right to make improvements to your home, but you must get the landlord's written agreement first.[16] If the landlord refuses you permission, you can challenge this in the County Court. It is the landlord's responsibility to prove that they are being reasonable. The landlord might, for example, argue that the work you propose would reduce the value or safety of the property. When landlords refuse permission they must give their reasons in writing. You can apply to the local council for a grant to help pay for the improvement (see page 138). The landlord cannot put up the rent because of improvements you have made.

THE RIGHT TO BE CONSULTED BY THE LANDLORD

Secure tenants (but not tenants of county councils) have a right to be consulted by their landlord on all matters of housing management which might substantially affect them.[17] This would cover, for example, repair programmes or caretaking arrangements, but does not include rent increases. Landlords are free to decide how to carry out these consultations and must publish details of how they will consult tenants. The details must be available for tenants to examine free of charge, and copies must be on sale at a reasonable cost. If new policies or practices are introduced without tenants being consulted, then the landlord is breaking the law. However, once they have consulted tenants, landlords are free to go ahead with their plans even if the tenants disagree.

CHANGES TO THE TENANCY AGREEMENT

All the rights described in this section are written into the Housing Act 1985. Landlords cannot reduce or remove them by anything that is put in your tenancy agreement. If they want to change your tenancy agreement they have to give you a written notice in advance, stating what changes they want to make and giving you a reasonable period in which to comment on them.[18] However, once they have consulted you, even if you disagree with the change, they can still go ahead with it. Once they decide to go ahead they must serve a *notice of variation* giving at least four weeks' notice of the change.

RIGHTS TO INFORMATION

Landlords must provide you with a simple written explanation of your rights under the Housing Act 1985 described in this section, and of their duties to carry out repairs.[19] They must also provide you with a written explanation of your rights and obligations under the tenancy agreement.

Landlords must publish a summary of the rules they apply in deciding who should be offered housing and which tenants should be offered transfers.[20] The full set of rules should be available at a reasonable charge. Landlords must provide anyone who asks with a free copy of a summary of the rules. You also have the right to check that any information you have given to the landlord about an application for housing or transfer has been accurately recorded.

THE RIGHT TO BUY

The best publicised of the rights of public sector tenants has been the right to buy.[21] Full details are available from your landlord. You have the right to buy the property of which you are a secure tenant if you have been a public sector tenant for at least two years. You need not necessarily have been a public sector tenant for this period in your present property. Time spent in other public sector properties counts as well.

You are entitled to a discount according to the length of time you have been a public sector tenant. The discount starts at 32 per cent of the value of the property for the first two years you have been a tenant with an extra one per cent discount for each additional year, up to a maximum of 60 per cent. If you are buying a flat rather than a house you are entitled to a higher discount, starting at 44 per cent and going up by two per cent for each additional year as a tenant up to 70 per cent. However, if you resell the property within the first three years after you buy it, you have to repay some of the discount, ranging from 100 per cent repayment if you sell in the first year to one third of the discount if you resell in the third year. The following do not have the right to buy:

- Housing Association tenants who are assured tenants (see page 79).
- Tenants of properties owned by charities, although some tenants of charities are entitled to a lump sum grant equivalent to the discount they would otherwise have received to help them buy on the open market. Ask your landlord for details.
- Tenants of sheltered housing for the elderly, physically disabled, mentally ill and mentally handicapped.
- Tenants of properties which are especially suitable for elderly people and which have previously been let to the elderly or disabled.

If you qualify for the right to buy there is also a right to a mortgage from the local council if you are a council tenant or from the Housing Corporation if you are a housing association tenant. But check first on mortgages from building societies and high street banks as they may be cheaper. If you cannot afford it immediately you can defer the purchase for two years and still buy at the original price. Alternatively, you can buy a part of the property on a shared ownership basis (see page 41 for an explanation of shared ownership) with the right to buy additional shares, up to full ownership, in the future.[22]

Before deciding to take up the right to buy, make sure that you know all the extra costs involved and that you can afford them now and in the future. In addition to mortgage payments you will have to pay rates, water rates, insurance, service charges if in a flat, and all repair and maintenance costs.

If you suffer a drop in income in future you may find there is no extra help available to meet your housing costs (see page 100).

COUNCIL TENANTS: CHANGE OF LANDLORD

Private landlords and housing associations have been given rights in the Housing Act 1988 to take over council estates.[23] If another landlord wishes to take over your estate, they must consult with the tenants. Tenants can only prevent it if more than half of all the tenants (not just of those voting) vote against the takeover. Tenants who do not vote will be counted as voting in favour of the transfer. However, even if a new landlord does take over the estate, individual tenants who want to keep the council as their landlord will be able to do so. Tenants who want to take over their own estate and run it as a co-operative will also be able to use this power to require the council to sell the estate to them. Contact the National Federation of Housing Co-ops for further advice (see *Useful addresses*).

In addition, local councils can agree voluntarily to transfer all or part of their housing stock to other landlords. In these cases, there is no obligation for the council to hold a ballot of tenants. However, the transfer has to be approved by the Department of the Environment and they should not allow it to go ahead if a majority of tenants affected oppose it.

6: **Housing rights and relationship break up**

When the relationship of a couple who have been married or living together breaks up, there are often problems over which of them has the right to live in the home. The rights of the partners depend on whether or not they are married, on the custody arrangements for any children and their legal status in the home. When a relationship breaks up there are many difficult personal decisions to be made. This chapter deals only with the housing aspects of the problems. For further advice on other problems, see Chapter 7 and the SHAC guides *A Woman's Place* (for married women) and *Going It Alone* (for unmarried women). Because it is usually women who suffer from domestic violence and the threat of the loss of their home after a relationship breaks up, this chapter refers throughout to women. However, the rights described here apply equally to men. Where action in connection with divorce is referred to this is shorthand not only for divorce proceedings but also for judicial separation and nullity proceedings.

In an emergency

If you are a women who lives with a man who threatens you or is violent to you or your children, you may need to take action quickly. The main possibilities are:

GOING TO A WOMEN'S REFUGE

See page 44 for details of these.

GOING TO THE COUNCIL

You can go to the council and ask for help as a homeless person. Local councils have duties under the Housing Act 1985 to help homeless people; see page 16 for further details. The government *Code of Guidance* which advises local authorities on how to perform their duties under the Act encourages them to help women in fear of violence. It says 'Authorities are asked to respond sympathetically to applications from women who are in fear of violence. The fact that violence has not yet occurred does not, on its own, suggest that it is not likely to occur'.[1]

However, some local councils demand proof of violence and you may need to get evidence from a professional person such as a doctor or social worker or from the police if they have been involved.

Some councils might say that you are not homeless or that they can discharge their duty to you because you could get a court order or *injunction* to protect you, even though these are often useless in preventing violence. Get advice if the local council is refusing to help you.

Even if you are not counted as being in *priority need* (see page 17), some councils will offer accommodation to all battered women, but there is no legal obligation on councils to do so.

The *Code of Guidance* states that a battered woman who has had to leave home because of violence or threats of violence should never be regarded as having become *intentionally homeless.*[2] Get advice if the council says that you are intentionally homeless.

If you are accepted as homeless by a local council away from your home area, it is not allowed to send you back to that area for housing if there is a risk of violence to you in that area.[3]

GETTING AN INJUNCTION

The other course of action you can take in an emergency is to get a court order against the man you live with. These orders are known as *injunctions* and can do a number of things. They can order a man:

— not to assault or harass you (this is known as a *non-molestation order)*;
— not to assault any children living with you;
— to leave the home and not to return (this is known as an *ouster*);
— to keep a certain distance from your home or any other place you or your children go regularly;
— to let you back into your home if he has excluded you.

If you believe a court order like this would help you, you should get advice immediately on where to find a solicitor or law centre. Your solicitor will be able to apply for an injunction under the Domestic Violence and Matrimonial Proceedings Act 1976. This Act applies equally whether or not you are married to the man you are living with. The courts regard exclusion orders, which forbid the man to enter the home, as very serious measures; particularly if the man owns the home where you are living, or if the tenancy is in his name only, it is that much more difficult to get anything more than a short-term exclusion order. In such cases, the court is likely to put a time limit on the injunction, probably of no more than three months. However, if you have the tenancy or ownership of the property in your name only you should be able to get a permanent exclusion order, and you may also be able to get a permanent order if you are joint tenants.

If the man disobeys the injunction, he is disobeying the court and is in *contempt of court*. This means that he can be brought back to court again and the judge can alter the terms of the injunction to try to make it more effective or can order that the man is imprisoned. It is likely, however, that the court will be willing on the first occasion to accept a promise of good conduct in the future. If the man is imprisoned he may be released after a short time if he apologises to the court for his behaviour.

An injunction is likely to be more effective if a *power of arrest* is attached to it. This can be done if the judge is satisfied that there has been actual bodily harm and that this is likely to happen again. The power of arrest enables the police to arrest the man without a warrant if they have reasonable cause to believe that he has disobeyed the injunction. If there is a power of arrest attached to the injunction, make sure that a copy of the injunction has been sent to the local police station so that they know in advance that they might have to take action. However, the police are not obliged to arrest the man even if there is further trouble and, indeed, they are often reluctant to become involved in domestic disputes.

If the problem is urgent, or you do not want the man to know that you are taking legal action because he is likely to become more violent, you can go straight to court without him being informed. This is known as an *ex parte* application. Because the man does not have an opportunity to put his case, the order will only be a temporary one until a full hearing can be arranged, in perhaps a week's time, where both sides can put their case. It is more difficult to get an exclusion order with an *ex parte* injunction unless there is very clear evidence of violence and courts are also reluctant to attach a power of arrest in such cases.

Other types of injunction

The Domestic Violence and Matrimonial Proceedings Act 1976 is the most straightforward way of getting an injunction. There are, however, other ways on which your solicitor can advise you. If you are married you can take similar action in the Magistrates' Court through the Domestic Proceedings and Magistrates' Court Act 1978, if there has been actual or threatened violence. If you are married and are already taking proceedings for divorce or judicial separation, it is possible to go to the court which is dealing with your case to ask for an injunction under the Matrimonial Homes Act 1983.

If you are not married to nor living with the man who is threatening you with violence, it is possible to take action against him for trespass, if he is entering your home without permission, and for assault. You can get an injunction ordering him to stop molesting you and also ask for damages against him.

Problems with injunctions
It may be that an injunction will help to protect you, but there are problems with them. They are usually only temporary; they cannot normally, for example, deprive the man permanently of any legal rights he might have to the home. Some men are not deterred by an injunction and may indeed be incited to further violence. Women are sometimes pressurised by local councils into applying for an injunction as an alternative to being housed by the council. No one has the right to insist that you apply for an injunction and, if this happens to you, you should get advice.

Long-term rights to the home.

Your long-term rights to stay in the home depend on whether or not you are married to your partner and on what are the present legal rights of each of you to the home.

IF YOU ARE MARRIED

If you are married and your *tenancy or ownership of the home is in joint names* you have equal rights to live in the home and, if it is owner occupied, to a share of the proceeds if it is sold. For this reason couples are usually best advised to have their tenancy or ownership in joint names. You may in certain circumstances (see below) have a right to more (or less) than a half share, or to the tenancy in your name after the divorce.

If you are married but the *ownership or tenancy is in one name only*, there are laws to protect the rights of the other partner.

The Married Women's Property Act 1882 gives a court power to decide who has ownership or rights over the matrimonial home even if the property is held in the name of only one person (usually the husband). The Act can also apply to people who have been married but are now divorced and to people who were planning to get married within three years of their engagement.

The Matrimonial Homes Act 1983 gives spouses who are not the owner or tenant of the home the right to live there and also gives the court the power to exclude either of the spouses, even if they are the sole or joint owner or tenant.

If your husband has left and stopped paying the rent or mortgage repayments, the landlord or building society is obliged to accept the payments from you (if you wish to make them) even though the home is not in your name. If your home is owned by your husband you can register your right to live in it. This prevents your husband selling the home before the court has decided who has a right to it and also prevents him from taking out a second mortgage on the property without your knowledge. This is known as *registering a charge* on the home. You should ask your solicitor to do it immediately. This Act also gives the court power to transfer a fully protected private tenancy (see page 52), an assured tenancy (see page 67) or a council or housing association secure tenancy (see page 79) from one partner to the other.

If the matrimonial home is owner occupied and proceedings have started for a divorce, then the court will use powers under the Matrimonial Causes Act 1973 and the Matrimonial and Family Proceedings Act 1984 to decide how the value of the property should be divided up. The law recognises that even if the home is in the husband's name only, the wife has a right to a share in its value, that she often makes a large unpaid contribution through housework and childcare and that this should be recognised in divorce proceedings. The court looks at a number of things to decide how much you should get. The Matrimonial and Family Proceedings Act 1984 states that first consideration must be given to any children of the marriage while they are under 18. After that, the court looks at:

- the income and resources of both you and your husband. This can include any income you are likely to have, or could reasonably be expected to get in the future. This means that the court may look at your future earning capacity and may consider that it is reasonable to expect you to go back to work in the future. It may be that you will have to provide evidence of the lack of employment opportunities in the area;
- the needs of you and your husband. This means what you need to live on, and what your husband's needs are (for example, if he has remarried and has a second family to support);
- the standard of living that you and your husband had before your marriage broke down;
- your ages, and how long the marriage lasted;
- any physical or mental disabilities affecting you or your husband;
- any contributions that you and your husband have made to the welfare of the family and any contributions that you are likely to make in the future.

This means, if you have custody of the children, the court will take into account the fact that you will be looking after the children for some years to come;

- the conduct of you and your husband. The behaviour of you and your husband will only be taken into account if the court thinks that it would be unfair to ignore it;

- the loss of any benefits that you might have had if the marriage had not broken down (for example any pension scheme that your husband may belong to).

The court also has to consider whether there is any way that they can make a 'clean break' between you and your husband. This means ensuring that there would be no further financial ties between you and your husband.

In certain circumstances the court can order the sale of the matrimonial home and the distribution of the money raised between the partners.

The court can also order that one partner has the right to live in the property indefinitely or for a particular period (for example, until a change of circumstances such as remarriage), after which it will be sold and the proceeds divided as the court decides. This is commonly used to ensure that a woman who has custody of the children has a home to bring them up in.

IF YOU ARE NOT MARRIED

If you are not married to your partner your rights depend on who is the tenant or owner of the home.

Tenants

Tenancy in your name alone: If you have a tenancy in your name alone, then your partner is probably only allowed to stay there in law as long as you permit it. If he refuses to leave after reasonable notice has been given to him, you can get a court order to evict him.

Tenancy in joint names: If you have a joint tenancy in both your names then you both have equal rights to the home. You can exclude your partner temporarily if he is violent or threatening violence by getting an injunction (see page 156). It is possible, although not usual, to get a court order to exclude him indefinitely from a joint tenancy. You will probably have to try to reach agreement on who should stay. If you are a council tenant you may be able to get the council to rehouse one of you. Get advice on rehousing by the council from an independent agency (see page 164). Do not just give up a tenancy as you may find the council will decide you are intentionally homeless and refuse to help you.

Tenancy in your partner's name: If the tenancy is in your partner's name alone then you have very limited rights to stay there. If there has been violence or the threat of violence, you can get the man excluded temporarily while you find another place to live (see *In an emergency*, page 155). Get advice immediately as, if your partner wants you to leave, you can apply to the local council as a homeless person. See page 16 to find out whether you might be entitled to rehousing by the council. If there is no violence, or your partner will not evict you, you will probably find it difficult to persuade the council to help you, and you should get advice.

Home Owners

If you live in an owner occupied home you and your partner may have certain rights to a share of the property even if you are not married. These rights have been established over many years in the courts, but there are no specific Acts of Parliament to protect you.

If the home is jointly owned: You have a clear right to a share in its value. If you have contributed equally towards buying and maintaining it then you would normally be entitled to a half-share, but if one of you has contributed more than the other that person may be entitled to more than a half. The court cannot order that the property is transferred to one partner or the other, but it has power under the Law of Property Act 1925 to order that it is sold so that each partner gets their share. However, if you want to stay in the property you could try to raise another mortgage to buy out your partner's share.

If your home is in your partner's name: You have no automatic right to live in the home even if the relationship has lasted a long time and there are children. However, you can get a solicitor to argue in court that the purpose of your partner in setting up the home was to provide for you and any children. You might also be able to show that you have contributed to the property either by helping with mortgage repayments or perhaps putting up money for a deposit, or by helping with maintenance or improvement of the property (but day-to-day housework does not count here). If any of these circumstances apply, you might be able to go to court to argue that your partner holds the property *on trust* for you. This will give you a right to a share in the value of the property that will be decided by the court. If you are going to court to argue this, you should make sure that your solicitor registers your claim on the property (see page 159) so that your partner cannot sell it before the case comes to court.

If the house is in your name only: The same points will apply as if the house was in your partner's name only (see above).

Money Problems

If your relationship is breaking up there are a number of money problems you might have to sort out.

- *Maintenance:* If you are *married* you can make an application for maintenance payments and for changes in the amount paid at any time during the marriage or after it is finished. Maintenance can be claimed for children and for yourself. The court considers the resources available to each partner and, most importantly, the needs of any children. Decisions over maintenance are tied up with decisions over the future of your home, because transfer of a tenancy or ownership of the home to you may form part of the arrangements for future maintenance and you might settle for a transfer of the home in return for lower money payments. Consult your solicitor, who will be concerned to get the best arrangement for you.

  If you are *not married* you can apply for maintenance for any children from their father, but cannot claim any maintenance payments for yourself.

- *Rent arrears:* If you or your partner have got into rent arrears then the responsibility for paying off the arrears will depend on who is the tenant. If the tenancy is in one name only then that person is responsible for the arrears and the other partner cannot be made to pay them off. So if, for example, the tenancy was in your husband's name only and he has run up arrears, you are not responsible for paying them off. If the tenancy is in *joint names* then you are both equally liable. If, however, you are the tenant of a public landlord such as a local authority or housing association, but in practice your partner took responsibility for paying the rent and ran up arrears without your knowledge, you could try asking your landlord to write off the arrears. They do not have to do this, but they may treat your problems sympathetically.

- *Mortgage arrears*: If you or your partner have run up mortgage arrears, read the advice on page 100.

- *Loss of income:* If you have suffered a loss of income because of the break up with your partner, you may well qualify for extra welfare benefits. Get advice and see *Useful publications.*

Custody of children

If you are *married*, decisions will have to be made about who will have custody of any children. This usually happens as part of the divorce proceedings, although if there is a dispute while you are still married you can apply to the court at any time for a decision on the upbringing of the children. People often worry that if they do not have an adequate home, or if the home is in their partner's name, they might not get custody of the children. But this should not affect your chances of custody because:

- The court awards custody according to its judgment of the best interests of the children. The most important factor is who is closest to them and best able to look after them and housing is only one point to be taken into account.
- The court will often decide to give you a right to stay in the matrimonial home because you are the best person to look after the children.
- If you are in danger of becoming homeless and have custody of the children, the local council may well have a responsibility to find a home for you (see page 16).

If you are *not married*, the mother has automatic custody of the children and, although this could be disputed by the father, it is only in very unusual cases that he would gain custody.

Key points to remember

- If your relationship is breaking up and your home is at risk get legal advice from a solicitor or law centre immediately. You may be able to get legal aid to help with the costs of this (see page 166).
- You may have a right to keep up rent and mortgage payments, even if the home is in your partner's name and he has left you.
- You may have a right to stay in the home either temporarily or permanently and to have it transferred to your name even if it is at present in your partner's name.

7: Getting advice and legal representation

This chapter tells you where to go for further advice and help. Addresses and telephone numbers of the organisations listed can be found in the appendix, *Useful addresses*.

General advice

- The nationwide network of **Citizens Advice Bureaux** provides advice on all problems including housing, legal matters, welfare benefits and relationship breakdown. If necessary, they can refer you for more detailed help to specialist agencies or to a solicitor. The advice service is free of charge. To find your local office look in the telephone directory under 'Citizens Advice Bureau' or telephone the National Association of Citizens Advice Bureaux.
- In some areas there are **neighbourhood centres** which offer free advice services often based in shops in high streets or shopping centres.

Housing advice centres

In many areas there are specialist centres offering housing aid and advice. The service they offer varies from one-off information to detailed help over a long period. There are two main types:

- **Local council housing aid centres** which can advise on all problems. However, they will not usually be able to take action against their own local council. If you have a problem with the local council, its housing aid centre may be able to discuss the matter with other sections of the council but will not, for example, be able to take legal action against it. So if you have a dispute with the council (for example, over repairs or because it will not accept you as a homeless person), you would probably do better to go to an independent advice centre.

- **Independent housing aid centres:** These can often offer detailed assistance over a period of time. These centres usually cover all types of housing problems and offer their services free of charge. There are a number of housing aid centres throughout the country operated by Shelter. In London you can contact SHAC (The London Housing Aid Centre) or, if you are without children, Housing Advice Switchboard.

Other specialist advice

- **Law Centres:** Law centres give free legal advice and sometimes can also represent you in court. They can usually advise on all aspects of housing law and can help with injunctions for battered women. They cannot, however, take on divorce cases, for which you will need a solicitor. To find out if there is a law centre in your area contact the Law Centres Federation.

- **Welfare rights:** For advice on welfare rights you can try your local council, who may employ a welfare rights officer. Advisers can also contact the Advice Line which is run by the Child Poverty Action Group. For general advice on social security from the DSS you can ring Freeline Social Security.

- **One parent families:** The National Council for One Parent Families can give advice to one parent families and single pregnant women on all problems, including housing, social security and divorce.

  Gingerbread is a national organisation for single parents, with local branches. It offers general advice and can refer on to specialist agencies.

- **Women's rights:** The Women's Aid Federation England and Welsh Women's Aid refer battered women (with or without children) to refuges. They give advice on injunctions, divorce, housing and social security. They can put you in touch with sympathetic solicitors and local women's aid groups.

  The Equal Opportunities Commission can give advice and help on action against sex discrimination.

- **Immigration:** The Joint Council for the Welfare of Immigrants (JCWI) offers advice and help on all types of problem concerned with immigration and nationality.

The United Kingdom Immigrants Advisory Service (UKIAS) offers advice and help on problems over immigration.

Many areas have local Community Relations Councils (CRCs) which can also help and advise. You can get the address of your local CRC from local advice centres.

○ **Racial discrimination:** The Commission for Racial Equality can give advice and help on action against racial discrimination, as can local Community Relations Councils.

Solicitors

Solicitors can advise you on all aspects of the law, represent you in certain courts and if necessary get a barrister to represent you. However, it is best to find a solicitor who specialises in the area of the law which is relevant to your problem (not all, for example, are equally expert on the law protecting private tenants, or equally expert at getting injunctions for battered women). You may be able to claim legal aid to cover all or part of the cost of the solicitor's services, so you will need one who operates the Legal Aid Scheme. If you do not know of a good solicitor, contact one of the advice agencies listed above and ask for a recommendation.

The Legal Aid Scheme

The Legal Aid Scheme can meet all or part of your legal costs. Not all solicitors operate the scheme, so ask an advice agency for one who does. There are two types of legal aid for non-criminal cases. The first type enables you to get initial advice and help and is called the *Green Form Scheme*. The second type is help under a *Legal Aid Certificate* which covers all types of costs including the cost of being represented in court if necessary.

THE GREEN FORM SCHEME

The official name for this is the *Legal Advice and Assistance Scheme*. Under the scheme you can get up to £50 worth of advice and assistance on practically any area of the law that is normally dealt with by a solicitor. The figure is increased to £90 in cases of undefended divorce or judicial separation.

The scheme can pay for the cost of your solicitor writing letters, negotiating on your behalf and obtaining advice from a barrister about your case. However, you cannot normally get help with the cost of taking a case to court or of representation at a court or tribunal, although under the scheme your solicitor can give you advice on how to conduct your case in person. In some cases advice over and above the cost limits of £50 and £90 can be obtained. Your solicitor will work out whether your income is low enough to qualify for help under this scheme. You may have to pay part of the cost yourself.

In addition, many solicitors also operate a fixed fee interview scheme under which anyone, regardless of their income, can get up to half an hour's advice for £5.

LEGAL AID UNDER A LEGAL AID CERTIFICATE

This covers all types of legal costs, including the cost of going to court. Your solicitor will help you fill in an application form. It will normally take some weeks for the application to be processed and it will not be possible to start court proceedings until the certificate is granted. However, in urgent cases, for example obtaining an injunction to exclude a violent partner from your home, an application for emergency legal aid can be made. In cases of extreme urgency, a solicitor can request an Emergency Certificate over the telephone.

To qualify for help, you have to pass two tests:

- You must come within the financial limits of the scheme which takes both income and savings into account. These are assessed by the DSS and the limits change fairly regularly. Your local advice centre should be able to give you an idea of whether you qualify and roughly what contribution, if any, you would have to make. If you are married and living with your spouse, and not in dispute with him or her, your income and capital will be added together in working out whether you qualify for help.

- You also have to have reasonable grounds for taking or defending the action. This will be decided by the Law Society who administer the scheme. They will not prejudge the rights and wrongs of your case, but simply decide whether it is reasonable to spend public funds on pursuing it.

THE LAW SOCIETY'S CHARGE

There is one particular feature of the legal aid scheme which it is vital for anybody who seeks legal aid to understand. If you succeed in recovering or retaining money or property (including for example, a house where there has been a dispute over who has the right to it) then you may, in addition to your initial contribution to the costs, if any, have to pay an extra sum for legal costs.

This extra sum is known as the Law Society's Charge and your solicitor has a duty to explain it to you fully.

In matrimonial cases special rules apply: the first £2,500 of a money or property settlement is exempt from the charge.

When it is property, rather than cash, that has been recovered or retained, the Law Society has discretion not to insist on immediate payment of the money due to them and to transfer the charge to a different property. It is the practice to wait until the house is sold before recovering the money or even, in some cases, to agree to transfer the charge to another house, which means it stays as an outstanding debt. This may be agreed if there is at least one dependent child who will be living with you in the second house, or if the reason for the move is to do with health, disability or employment and a refusal would cause hardship. Obviously, the equity in the second house must be sufficient to cover the amount owed to the Law Society.

There have been a number of very sad cases in recent years where people on legal aid have been involved in a prolonged and expensive dispute over property and in the end have been left with very little of the sum awarded to them because of the way in which the Law Society's Charge operates. It is always worth making every effort to negotiate a settlement prior to a court hearing rather than fight the matter out in court because of the large extra costs for which you might become liable.

Campaigning to change policies

Housing problems are not only tackled by individual action, indeed in some circumstances you may be able to solve your own problem more quickly and effectively by collective rather than individual action. One example is the problem of getting local councils to do repairs, where tenants' associations can often have far more impact than any individual. You may wish to share your experiences with other people who have had similar problems, or help to campaign for better housing policies whether from local councils or the government. This section gives you information on campaigning organisations you can contact. Their addresses and telephone numbers are listed in the section *Useful addresses*.

COUNCIL TENANTS

Contact your local tenants' association.

PRIVATE TENANTS

Contact a local tenants' or residents' association if there is one.

Houses in multiple occupation

There is a growing campaign locally and nationally for better enforcement of the laws on conditions in HMOs and for new laws to improve conditions. For details contact the Campaign for Bedsit Rights.

SINGLE PEOPLE

CHAR is the housing campaign for single people. It advises charities working in this field, represents the interests of single people in negotiations with central and local government and researches and disseminates information about single people and their conditions and needs. CHAR does not provide accommodation or advice to individuals.

WELFARE RIGHTS

Child Poverty Action Group (CPAG) researches and campaigns on poverty and welfare rights. Individuals and groups can join as members of CPAG.

GENERAL CAMPAIGNS

Shelter is the national campaign for homeless people. It sponsors housing aid centres and special projects to help the homeless and badly housed as well as undertaking campaigning and research on housing issues. Individuals and groups can join as members of Shelter.

SHAC (The London Housing Aid Centre) undertakes research, policy and campaigning work on a range of housing issues in addition to its housing aid and training work.

Appendix I Useful publications

Publications listed here can be obtained either through bookshops or, particularly in the case of those produced by voluntary organisations, directly from the publishers. Booklets produced by the Department of the Environment (listed as DoE *Housing booklets*) are available free from advice centres.

GENERAL HOUSING LAW

For greater detail on housing law generally the following are highly recommended:

Manual of Housing Law, Andrew Arden (Sweet and Maxwell)

For housing advisers, lawyers and others with some familiarity with housing law this is an indispensable handbook for everyday reference.

Housing Law, Andrew Arden and Martin Partington (Sweet and Maxwell)

A detailed and definitive textbook on housing law for lawyers and experienced housing advisers who need to explore the intricacies of the law.

Encyclopaedia of Housing Law and Practice, general editor Andrew Arden (Sweet and Maxwell)

Four large volumes of all relevant legislation, rules, orders and circulars, regularly updated. Legislation and regulations are frequently amended in an extremely complex way. Anyone wishing to check on the current state of the law will find this encyclopaedia indispensable. It also incorporates detailed explanatory commentary.

CHAPTER 1

Homeless Persons — The Housing Act 1985 Part III Andrew Arden (Legal Action Group)

Detailed commentary on the homelessness legislation, Code of Guidence and cases.

Homelessness: A digest of court decisions (Housing Aid Trust)

With an annual updating service.

In on the Act (CHAR)

A guide to the Homeless Persons Act for single people.

The New Towns

Free booklet from The New Towns Association.

Co-op Outlines (The Housing Corporation)
A series of leaflets giving information and advice for people thinking of setting up a co-op.
Setting up a Housing Co-op (Kilburn and Cyron Housing Co-ops, 1a Beethoven Street, London W10)
Directory of Housing Co-ops (National Federation of Housing Co-ops)
Buying a Home (SHAC)
Building Societies and House Purchase (Building Societies Association)
The Conveyancing Fraud Michael Joseph
Published by Michael Joseph, 27 Occupation Lane, London SE18.
Reveals how little work solicitors do for their large conveyancing fees and tells you how to do it yourself.
Do it yourself Conveyancing Robert T. Steele (David and Charles)
Shared Ownership (Housing Corporation)
Free leaflet on housing association shared ownership schemes.
Somewhere to Stay (National Council for One Parent Families).
A directory of short stay accommodation for single pregnant women and lone parents.
Filling the Empties: Short Life Housing and How to do it (Shelter)
The London Hostels Directory (Resource Information Service)
Squatters' Handbook (Advisory Service for Squatters)
Racial Discrimination — a guide to the Race Relations Act 1976 (The Home Office)
Race Relations Rights Paul Gordon, John Wright, Patricia Hewitt (NCCL)
Guide to the Race Relations Act with tactical advice on taking up a case.
Local Government and Racial Equality (Commission for Racial Equality)
Guidance to local authorities on meeting their duty to promote racial equality.
Sex Discrimination — A Guide to the Sex Discrimination Act 1975 (The Home Office)

CHAPTER 2

Security of Tenure in the Private Rented Sector (Association of Housing Aid)
An excellent manual for advisers.
Notice to Quit (DoE Housing Booklet No. 11)
Shorthold Tenancies (DoE Housing Booklet No. 8)
Assured Tenancies (DoE Housing Booklet No. 17)
Leasehold Reform (DoE Housing Booklet No. 9)
Mobile Homes (DoE Housing Booklet No. 16)
Squatters' Handbook (Advisory Service for Squatters)
The Private Tenant's Handbook Andrew Arden (Allison and Busby)

The Public Tenant's Handbook Andrew Arden (Allison and Busby)

CHAPTER 3

Owning your Flat — A Guide to Problems with your lease and landlord (SHAC)
Service Charges in Flats (DoE Housing Booklet No. 10)
Housing Association Rents (DoE Housing Booklet No. 13)
Rights Guide for Home Owners (SHAC/CPAG)
Detailed guide to cutting mortgage costs, increasing income and tackling mortgage arrears.
Guide to Housing Benefit Martin Ward and John Zebedee (SHAC and Institute of Housing)
Housing and Supplementary Benefits — A Rights Guide for Single Homeless People (CHAR)
A detailed guide for homeless people and hostel residents.
Rights Guide to Non-means-tested Social Security Benefits (CPAG)
National Welfare Benefits Handbook (CPAG)
Comprehensive guide to means-tested benefits.

CHAPTER 4

Your Rights to Repair: A Guide for Council Tenants Ken Baublys (SHAC)
Your Rights to Repair: A Guide for Private and Housing Association Tenants Ken Baublys (SHAC)
Effects of Defects David Ormandy (Shelter)
A checklist of defects that can be found in houses and their effects.
Public Health Practice Notes (Shelter)
1. Statutory nuisance and Section 99
2. Unfitness
3. Overcrowding
Procedures for dealing with bad housing conditions.
Repairs: Tenants' Rights, Jan Luba (Legal Action Group)
Home Improvement Grants (DoE Housing Booklet No. 14)

CHAPTER 5

The Fuel Rights Handbook (SHAC)
See also the publications under General Housing Law above.

CHAPTER 6

A Women's Place: A Guide for Married Women (SHAC)
Going It Alone: A Guide for Unmarried Women (SHAC)

The Cohabitation Handbook: A Women's Guide to the Law Anne Bottomley, Katherine Gieve, Gay Moon and Angela Weir (Pluto Press)
Divorce — Legal Procedurers and Financial Facts (Consumers' Association)
Matrimonial Property and Finance Peter Duckworth (Oyez Longman)
A detailed reference book.

CHAPTER 7
Tenants' Action
A guide for council tenants, including how to start a tenants' association. Free from Thames T.V. Help programme.
Framework for a Tenants' Charter (Community Projects Foundation)
Describes how Newcastle Tenants' Federation negotiated a Tenants' Charter. A useful model for other tenants' groups.
Housing and Campaigning (Shelter)
Using the Media Denis MacShane (Pluto Press)
How to use the media for campaigning.

ELDERLY PEOPLE
Your Housing in Retirement Janice Casey (Age Concern)
Staying Put or Moving on?
Guide for elderly home owners. Free from Thames T.V. Help Programme.
Guide to Services for the Ethnic Elderly (Commission for Racial Equality)
Your home in retirement (DoE)

PEOPLE WITH DISABILITIES
The Disability Rights Handbook (Disability Alliance)

Appendix II Useful addresses

Advisory Service for Squatters, 2 St Paul's Road, London N1, Tel: 01-359 8814

Age Concern, England, Bernard Sunley House, 60 Pitcairn Road, Mitcham, Surrey CR4 3LL, Tel: 01-640 5431

Association of Housing Aid, c/o Brent Housing Aid Centre, Robert Owen House, 192 High Road, London NW10, Tel: 01-451 0911

British Council for Aid to Refugees, Bondway House, 3-9 Bondway, London SW8

British Insurance Brokers Association, Fountain House, 130 Fenchurch Street, London EC3, Tel: 01-623 9043

Building Societies Association, 3 Savile Row, London W1X 1AF, Tel: 01-437 0655

Campaign for Bedsit Rights, 5-15 Cromer Street, London WC1H 8LS, Tel: 01-278 0598

CHAR, 5-15 Cromer Street, London WC1H 8LS, Tel: 01-833 2071

Child Poverty Action Group, (CPAG), 1-5 Bath Street, London EC1V 9PY Tel: 01-253 3406. Advice Line (for advisers only): 01-253 6569

Commission for Local Administration in England, 21 Queen Anne's Gate, London SW1H 9BU, Tel: 01-222 5622 (the local government ombudsman)

Commission for Racial Equality, Elliot House, 10-12 Allington Street, London SW1 5EH, Tel: 01-828 7022

Community Projects Foundation, 60 Highbury Grove, London N5 2AG

Consumers' Association, 14 Buckingham Street, London WC2, Tel: 01-839 1222

Corporation of Mortgage Brokers, 24 Broad Street, Wokingham, Berkshire

Department of the Environment, 2 Marsham Street, London SW1 3EB, Tel: 01-212 3434

Department of Social Security (DSS), Alexander Fleming House, Elephant and Castle, London SE1 6BY, Tel: 01-407 5522. DSS Freephone: free advice and information on welfare benefits, Tel: 0800 666555

Disability Alliance, 25 Denmark Street, London WC2H 8NJ, Tel: 01-240 0806

Electricity Consumers' Council, Brook House, 2-16 Torrington Place, London WC1, Tel: 01-636 5703

Empty Property Unit, 88 Old Street, London EC1V 9AX, Tel: 01-253 0202

Equal Opportunities Commission, Overseas House, Quay Street, Manchester M3 3HN, Tel: 061-833 9244

Ethnic Switchboard, Tel: 01-993 6119

Federation of Black Housing Organisations, 259a High Road, London N15 5BT, Tel: 01-802 7490

Federation of Claimants' Unions, 296 Bethnal Green Road, London E2, Tel: 01-739 4173

Freeline Social Security — see Department of Social Security

Gay Switchboard, Tel: 01-837 7324

Gingerbread, 35 Wellington Street, London WC2, Tel: 01-240 0953

HALO (Housing Association Liaison Office), 189a Old Brompton Road, London SW5 OAR, Tel: 01-370 6591/01-373 2005

Help the Aged, St. James's Walk, London EC1R 0BE, Tel: 01-253 0253

The Home Office, 50 Queen Anne's Gate, London SW1, Tel: 01-213 3000

Housing Advice Switchboard, 47 Charing Cross Road, London WC2, Tel: 01-434 2522 (telephone enquiries only)

Housing aid centres

England

South-East

Wellington House, 14-16 Church Road, Ashford, Kent, TN23 1RE, Tel: 0233-610669. Opening Hours: M-F: 9.30-5.30. Area covered: Kent, Sussex, Surrey, South Essex, Outside of Greater London

Hastings, Station Appts., Warrior Square Station, St. Leonards on Sea, East Sussex TN37 6HL, Tel: 0424-438075 (446573). Opening Hours: 9-1, 2-5; W: 9-1. Area covered: Rother DC; Hastings BC areas.

Southern Counties

85 Windsor Road, Slough SL1 2JL, Berks, Tel: 0753-691844 (692832). Opening Hours: M,T,F: 10-1, 2-5; W, Th, 10-1.30. Area covered: Berkshire, Buckinghamshire, Hampshire, East Dorset.

Portsmouth Community Advice Centre, W.E.A. Centre, New Road, Portsmouth, Tel: 0705-663233. Opening Hours: M-F; 10-1. Areas covered: Portsmouth area.

Milton Keynes, 510 Silbury Boulevard, Saxon Gate East, Central MK, MK9 3AF, Tel: 0908-667599 (663631) (663520). Opening Hours: M,T,F: 10-4; W, Th: 10-1.30. Area covered: Borough of MK. Surgeries at Wolverton & Bletchley CABs, Newport Pagnell & Olney Libraries.

Eastern Counties

21 Shoplands, Welwyn Garden City, Herts, Tel: 0707-320001 (329267). Opening Hours: M-F: 9.30-4.30. Area covered: Herts, North Essex, Cambs, Norfolk, Suffolk, South Beds.

Colchester Ind. Housing Aid Service, Winsleys House, High Street, Colchester, Essex, Tel: 0206-760426. Opening Hours: M-F: 9.15-4.15. Area covered: Colchester.

St. Albans District Council Offices, Civic Centre, St Peter's Street, St Albans, Herts. AL1 3JE, Tel: 0727-64010. Opening Hours: M-F: 9.30-12.30. Areas covered: St. Albans & District.

Bedfordshire, 6a Tavistock Place, Bedford MK40 2RY, Tel: 0234-328488. Opening Hours: M-F: 11-5 by appointment only. Area covered: Bedfordshire.

South-West
1 Mark Lane, Bristol BS1 4XR, Tel: 0272-268115 (268617). Opening Hours: M,W,Th,F: 10-1, 2-5; Tu: 2-5. Area covered: Avon, Wiltshire, Gloucestershire.

Cheltenham, 67 Clarence Street, Cheltenham, Glos GL50 3LB, Tel: 0242-573407. Opening Hours: W: 9.30-5. Area covered: Gloucestershire.

Devon & Cornwall, Virginia House, Palace Street, Plymouth PL4 OEQ, Tel: 0752-221187. Opening Hours: M,T,Th,F: 9.30-1; W:2-5. Area covered: Devon & Cornwall, Isles of Scilly.

Somerset, Castle Moat Chambers, Corporation Street., Taunton TA1 4AW, Tel: 0823-259961/2 (282457). Opening Hours: M-F: 10-1; Th, F: 2-5.30. Area covered: Somerset, W. Dorset & Weymouth.

West Midlands
Room 30, 2nd Flr. Ruskin Buildings, 191 Corporation Street, Birmingham, West Midlands, Tel: 021-236 6668 (6373). Opening Hours: M,T,Th,F: 9.30-1, 2-5.30; W: 2-5.30. Area covered: W. Mids., Staffs, Shrops, Hereford & Worcester, Warwicks, South Derbyshire.

Leicestershire, 13 Welford Road, Leicester LE2 7AD, Tel: 0533-546064. Opening Hours: M-F: 1-4. Area covered: Leicestershire, part of Lincolnshire, Northamptonshire, South Derbyshire.

Nottingham, 5 Queen's Chambers, King Street, Nottingham NG1 2BH, Tel: 0602-480479 (480474). Opening Hours: M-F: 9.30-5. Area covered: Nottinghamshire, Derbyshire, Lincolnshire.

Mansfield, St. Peters Chambers, 2 Churchside, Mansfield, Tel: 0623-659737 (659746). Opening Hours: M,T,W: 10-4; Th: 10-12. Area covered: Mansfield, Nth Nottinghamshire.

North-West
Rm 278-280 Corn Exchange Bdgs, Hanging Ditch, Manchester M4 3BP, Tel: 061-834 4809 (8456) 061-835 2442. Opening Hours: 9.30-5.30 except W. Area covered: Greater Manchester, Merseyside, Cumbria, Lancs.

Cleveland, 19-19a Borough Road, Middlesbrough, Cleveland, Tel: 0642-226616. Opening hours: M-F: 8.30-5. Area covered: Middlesbrough and Langbaurgh. *Housing and Welfare Rights Service for pensioners — MSC funded. **Casework and translation: Urdu & Punjabi.

Hartlepool, 38 Avenue Road, Hartlepool, Cleveland TS24 8AT, Tel: 0429-233725. Opening Hours: M-F: 8.30-5. Area covered: Hartlepool, Easington, Peterlee.

Stockton, 60 Yarm Lane, Stockton-on-Tees, Cleveland, Tel: 0642-226616. Opening Hours: 9-5. Area covered: Local area.

Tyneside, 1 Charlotte Square, Newcastle-upon-Tyne NE1 4XF, Tel: 091-2323778 (2328133) Opening Hours: Under review (2-5 emergencies). Area covered: Tyne & Wear, Durham, Northumberland.

Hull, 83-93 George Street, Hull, Humberside, Tel: 0482-29591 (29754). Opening hours: M,W,F: 10-4.30; T,Th: 10-1. Area covered: Humberside, part of Lincolnshire.

Wales

Swansea, 57 Walter Road, Swansea, West Glamorgan, Tel: 0792-464965. Opening Hours: T-F: 11-1, 2-4. Area covered: West & South Glamorgan, Dyfed, Powys.

Rhondda, 93 Tylycelyn Road, Penygraig, Rhondda, Mid Glam CF40 1LA, Tel: 0443-431004 (431029). Opening Hours: T-F: 11-1, 2-4. Area covered: Mid Glamorgan, Gwent.

Wrexham, 13 Lambpitt Street, Wrexham, Clwyd, Tel: 0978-363745 (357175). Opening Hours: T,W,Th,F: 10-3. Area covered: Wrexham Maelor Borough Council, Clwyd (will take enquiries N. Wales).

Aberystwyth, P.O. Box 29, Aberystwyth, Dyfed, Tel: 0970-617788. Opening hours: Limited. Area covered: Gwynedd.

The Housing Corporation, England: 149 Tottenham Court Road, London W1P 0BN, Tel: 01-387 9466; Wales: 24 Cathedral Road, Cardiff CF1 9LJ, Tel: 0222-384611.

Joint Council for the Welfare of Immigrants, 115 Old Street, London EC1V 9JR, Tel: 01-251 8706.

Law Centres

Law Centres Federation, Duchess House, 18-19 Warren Street, London W1P 5DB, Tel: 01-387 8570.

Adamsdown Law Centre, 15 Splott Road, Splott, Cardiff, Tel: 0222-498117.

Avon & Bristol Law Centre, 62 Bedminster Parade, Bristol BS8 4HL, Tel: 0272-667933.

Belfast Law Centre, 7 University Road, Belfast BT7 1NA, Tel: 0232-321307.

Bradford Law Centre, 31 Manor Row, Bradford BD1 4PX, Tel: 0274-306617.

Brent Law Centre, 190 High Road, Willesden, London NW10, Tel: 01-451 1122.

Brent Young People's Law Centre, 272 Willesden High Road, London NW10, Tel: 01-451 2428.

Brighton Law Centre, 36a Duke Street, Brighton BN1 1AG, Tel: 0273-29634.

Brixton Law Centre, 506-8 Brixton Road, London SW9, Tel: 01-733 4245.

Camden Community Law Centre, 2a Prince of Wales Road, London NW5 3LG, Tel: 01-485 6672.

Central London Law Centre, c/o 18-19 Warren Street, London W1P 5DB, Tel: 01-437 5854.

Coventry Legal & Income Rights Service, The Bridge, Broadgate, Coventry CV1 1NG, Tel: 0203-23051.

Dudley Law Centre, 96a High Street, Dudley DY1 1QP, W. Midlands, Tel: 0384-239243.

Ealing Law Centre, Steyne Hall, Rectory Road, London W3, Tel: 01-993 7801.

Gateshead Law Centre, Swinburne House, Swinburne Street, Gateshead, Tyne & Wear NE8 1AX, Tel: 091-477 1109.

Gloucester Law Centre, Widden Old School, Widden Street, Gloucester GL1 4AQ, Tel: 0452-423492.

Greenwich Law Centre, 187 Trafalgar Road, London SE10, Tel: 01-853 2550.

Hackney Law Centre, 236-8 Mare Street, London E8, Tel: 01-986 8446.

Hammersmith and Fulham Law Centre, 106-8 King Street, London W6, Tel: 01-741 4021 (telephone appointments only).

Handsworth Law Centre, 220 Soho Road, Birmingham 21, Tel: 021-554 0868.

Harehills and Chapeltown Law Centre, 263 Roundhay Road, Leeds LS8 4HS, Tel: 0532-491100.

Highfields and Belgrave Law Centre, Seymour House, 6 Seymour St, Highfields, Leicester, Tel: 0533-532928.

Hillingdon Legal Resource Centre, 12 Harold Avenue, Hayes, Middlesex UB3 4QW, Tel: 01-561 9440.

Hounslow Law Centre, 51 Lampton Road, Hounslow, Middlesex, Tel: 01-570 9505.

Hyson Green Law Centre, 65 Birkin Avenue, Hyson Green, Nottingham NG7 5AW, Tel: 0602-787813.

Leicester Rights Centre, 6 Bishop Street, Leicester LE1 6AF, Tel: 0533-553781.

Liverpool 8 Law Centre, 34-36 Princes Road, Liverpool 8, Tel: 051-709 7222.

Manchester Law Centre (North), Community Services Centre, Paget Street, Manchester 10 7UX, Tel: 061-205 5040.

Manchester Law Centre, (South Manchester Law Centre), 584 Stockport Road, Manchester 13 ORQ, Tel: 061-225 5111.

Middlesborough Law Centre, St Mary's Centre, 82-90 Corporation Road, Middlesborough, Cleveland TS1 2RW, Tel: 0642-223813/7.

Newcastle Law Centre, 85 Adelaide Terrace, Newcastle upon Tyne NE4 8BB, Tel: 091-273 1210.

Newham Rights Centre, 285 Romford Road, London E7, Tel: 01-555 3331.

North Islington Law Centre, 161 Hornsey Road, London N7, Tel: 01-607 2461.

North Kensington Law Centre, 74 Golborne Road, London W10, Tel: 01-969 7473.

North Lambeth Law Centre, 381 Kennington Lane, London SE11 5QY, Tel: 01-582 4425/4373.

North Lewisham Law Centre, 28 Deptford High Street, London SE8, Tel: 01-692 5355.

Paddington Law Centre, 439 Harrow Road, London W10 4RE, Tel: 01-960 3155.

Plumstead Law Centre, 105 Plumstead High Street, London SE18, Tel: 01-855 9817.

Roehampton and Putney Law Centre, 162 Upper Richmond Road, London SW15 2SL, Tel: 01-789 8232.

Salford Law Centre, 498 Liverpool Street, Salford M5, Tel: 061-736 3116.

Saltley Action Centre, 2 Alum Rock Road, Birmingham 8, Tel: 021-328 2307.

Sheffield Law Centre, 1st Floor, Yorkshire House, Leopold Street, Sheffield S1 2GZ, Tel: 0742-731888.

Small Heath Law Centre, 590a Coventry Road, Birmingham 10, Tel: 021-773 8121.

South Islington Law Centre, 131-2 Upper Street, London N1, Tel: 01-354 0133.

Southall Community Law Centre, Unit 2, Dilloway Lane, The Green, Southall, Middlesex UB2 4TD, Tel: 01-574 2434.

Southwark Law Centre, 29 Lordship Lane, London SE22, Tel: 01-299 1024.

Springfield Legal Advice Project, Springfield Hospital, Glenburnie Road, London SW17, Tel: 01-767 6884 (legal and welfare benefits advice primarily for patients of Springfield Hospital).

Stockton Law Centre, Old Town Hall, Mandale Road, Thornaby, Cleveland TS17 6HW, Tel: 0642-605060.

Stockwell and Clapham Law Centre, 337 Wandsworth Road, London SW8, Tel: 01-720 6231.

Thamesdown Law Centre, 26 Victoria Road, Swindon, Wilts, Tel: 0793-486926/7

Tooting and Balham Law Centre, 107 Trinity Road, London SW17, Tel: 01-672 8749.

Tottenham Law Centre, 15 West Green Road, London N15, Tel: 01-802 0911.

Tower Hamlets Law Centre, 341 Commercial Road, London E1, Tel: 01-791 0741.

Wandsworth Law Centre, 248 Lavender Hill, London SW11, Tel: 01-228 9462.

Warrington Community Law Centre, 64-66 Bewesey Street, Warrington, Cheshire, Tel: 0925-51104.

West Hampstead Law Centre, 59 Kingsgate Road, London NW6, Tel: 01-328 4501/4523.

Wolverhampton Law Centre, 2-3 Bell Street, Wolverhampton WV1 3PR, Tel: 0902-771122.

Wythenshawe Law Centre, Fenside Road, Sharston, Manchester M22 4WZ, Tel: 061-428 5929.

Legal Action Group, 242-244 Pentonville Road, London N1 9UN.

London Mutual Exchange Bureau, Devonshire House, 164-168 Westminster Bridge Road, London SE1 7RW, Tel: 01-928 8081.

Mental Health Advice Centre, 19 Handen Road, London SE12, Tel: 01-318 1330/1339

National Association of Citizens' Advice Bureaux (NACAB), Myddleton House, 115-123 Pentonville Road, London N1 9LZ, Tel: 01-833 2181.

National Association of Conveyancers, 2-4 Chichester Rents, Chancery Lane, London WC2.

National Association of Voluntary Hostels, 33 Long Acre, London WC2, Tel: 01-836 0193.

National Council for Civil Liberties, 21 Tabard Street, London SE1, Tel: 01-403 3888.

National Council for One Parent Families, 255 Kentish Town Road, London NW5 2LX, Tel: 01-267 1361.

National Federation of Housing Co-ops, 88 Old Street, London, EC1V 9AX, Tel: 01-608 2494.

The New Towns Association, Metro House, 57-58 St. James's Street, London SW1A 1LD.

New towns:

Aycliffe, Churchill House, Aycliffe, County Durham LD5 4LE.

Basildon, Gifford House, Basildon, Essex SS13 2EX.

Bracknell, Farley Hall, Bracknell, Berkshire RG12 5EU.

Central Lancashire, Cuerdon Hall, Bamber Bridge, Preston, Lancashire PR5 6AX.

Cwmbran, Gwent House, Town Centre, Cwmbran, Gwent NP44 1HZ.

Milton Keynes, Wavendon Tower, Wavendon, Milton Keynes MK17 8LX.

Newtown, Ladywell House, Newtown, Powys SY16 1UJ.

Northampton, Cliftonville House, Bedford Road, Northampton NN4 0AY.

Peterborough, Touthill Close, City Road, Peterborough PE1 1UJ.

Peterlee, Lee House, Peterlee, County Durham SR8 1BB.

Redditch, Holmwood, Plymouth Road, North Redditch, Worcestershire B97 4PD.

Runcorn, Chapel Street, Runcorn, Cheshire WA7 5AR.

Skelmersdale, Pennylands Skelmersdale, Lancashire WN8 8AR.

Telford, Priorslee Hall, Telford, Shropshire TF2 9NT.

Warrington, PO Box 49, New Town House, Buttermarket Street, Warrington WA1 2LF.

Washington, Usworth Hall, Stephenson District 12, Washington, Tyne & Wear NE37 3HS.

Pensioners Link (formerly Task Force), 17 Balfe Street, London N1 9EB, Tel: 01-278 5501/2/3/4.

Prisoners' Wives and Families Society, 254 Caledonian Road, London N1, Tel: 01-278 3981.

Resource Information Service, 5 Egmont House, 116 Shaftesbury Avenue, London W1V 7DJ, Tel: 01-494 2408.

Rights of Women, 52-54 Featherstone Street, London EC1, Tel: 01-251 6577.

The Royal Association for Disability and Rehabilitation (RADAR), 25 Mortimer Street, London W1N 8AB, Tel: 01-637 5400.

Shelter, 88 Old Street, London EC1V 9AX, Tel: 01-253 0202.

Tenants Exchange Scheme, PO Box 170, London SW1P 3PX.

Thames TV Help Programme, 149 Tottenham Court Road, London W1P 9LL, Tel: 01-388 5199.

U.K. Immigration Advisory Service, 7th Floor, Bretton House, Savoy Street, Strand WC2 7EH.

Welsh Women's Aid, Incentive House, Adam Street, Cardiff, Tel: 0222-462291/462683.

Women's Aid Federation England, 52-54 Featherstone Street, London EC1T 8RY, (Temporary) Tel: 01-251 6537 (24 hour) 01-251 6538/01-253 2033 (Office hours).

Notes on the law

These notes refer to the numbers in the text. They provide references for people who wish to check on legislation and government regulations and circulars. They refer only to the most important of these and are not intended to be comprehensive. References are not given where it is expected that expert legal advice will be sought. References to case law have not been included and people who wish to follow up these should refer to the legal books recommended in *Useful publications.*

Acts of Parliament are often amended by subsequent legislation and all references here are to legislation as amended up to January 1989. Full texts of amended legislation can be found in the *Encyclopaedia of Housing* (see *Useful publications).*

Acts of Parliament are divided into numbered *sections* and often have numbered *schedules* at the end. Section numbers are indicated by an *s* and schedule numbers by *Sch.* The government also makes regulations by Statutory Instruments and these are abbreviated to S.I., followed by the date and number of each one.

The following abbreviations are used:

CLA 1977 — Criminal Law Act 1977
CoG — Housing (Homeless Persons Act) 1977, Code of Guidance, 2nd Edition, 1983
HA 1980 — Housing Act 1980
HA 1985 — Housing Act 1985
HA 1988 — Housing Act 1988
HBR 1987 — The Housing Benefit (General) Regulations (S.I. 1987 No. 1971)
LCA 1973 — Land Compensation Act 1973
LTA 1954 — Landlord and Tenant Act 1954
LTA 1985 — Landlord and Tenant Act 1985
LTA 1987 — Landlord and Tenant Act 1987
MHA 1983 — Mobile Homes Act 1983
PEA 1977 — Protection from Eviction Act 1977
PHA 1936 — Public Health Act 1936
PHA 1961 — Public Health Act 1961
R(A)A 1976 — Rent (Agriculture) Act 1976
RA 1977 — Rent Act 1977
RRA 1976 — Race Relations Act 1976
SDA — Sex Discrimination Act 1975

So, for example, HA 1985 s. 84 and Sch. 2, Part 1 refers to the Housing Act 1985, section 84 and Schedule 2, Part 1.

Chapter 1

1 HA 1985 s. 106
2 London Government Act 1963 s. 22
3 HA 1985 s. 58

4 HA 1985 s. 59
5 CoG, para 2.12
6 HA 1985 s. 60
7 HA 1985 ss. 65-66
8 HA 1985 ss. 65-66
9 HA 1985 ss. 67-68
10 HA 1985 s. 74
11 HA 1985 s. 63
12 HA 1985 s. 64
13 HA 1985 s 70
14 LCA 1973 s. 39
15 LCA 1973 ss. 29, 30, 32, 37, 38
16 HA 1985 ss. 578-603, Sch. 23 and 24
17 HA 1985 s. 104
18 HA 1985 s. 106
19 HA 1985 s. 92 and Sch. 3
20 Accommodation Agencies Act 1953
21 HA 1985 s. 106
22 HA 1980 ss. 88-89 and Sch. 25, para. 61
23 RRA 1976 ss. 1-2
24 RRA 1976 ss.1-2
25 RRA 1976 s. 24
26 RRA 1976 s. 22
27 RRA 1976 s. 21
28 RRA 1976 s. 71
29 RRA 1976 s. 20
30 SDA 1975 ss. 1, 2 and 4
31 SDA 1975 ss. 29-30
32 SDA 1975 s. 29.

Chapter 2

1 RA 1977 ss. 4-16A
2 RA 1977 s. 24
3 RA 1977 ss. 21-22
4 RA 1977 s. 2
5 HA 1957 ss. 22(5) and 27(5)
6 RA 1977 s. 101
7 PEA 1977 s. 5
8 Notices to Quit (Prescribed Information) Regulations, 1980 S.I. 1980 No. 1624
9 RA 1977 Sch. 15, Part I
10 RA 1977 s. 98
11 RA 1977 Sch. 15, Part IV
12 RA 1977 Sch. 15, Part I
13 RA 1977 ss. 19-21
14 RA 1977 ss. 102A-106

15 RA 1977 s. 106A
16 HA 1980 ss. 53-55
17 PEA 1977 s. 8(2)
18 R(A)A 1976 s. 2 and Sch. 3
19 R(A)A 1976 s.4
20 R(A)A 1976 Sch. 2
21 R(A)A 1976 Sch. 4
22 R(A)A 1976 ss. 27-29
23 PEA 1977 s. 4
24 HA 1980 ss. 56-58
25 HA 1988 s. 34
26 HA 1988 Sch. 1
27 HA 1988 ss. 1-7
28 HA 1988 s. 8
29 HA 1988 s. 7
30 HA 1988 Sch. 2
31 HA 1988 ss. 20-21
32 HA 1988 s. 31
33 HA 1988 ss. 24-26
34 PEA 1977 s. 5
35 RA 1977 Sch. 15, Part 1, Case 6
36 RA 1977 s. 137
37 HA 1988 s. 18
38 RA 1977 s. 19
39 HA 1980 s. 89
40 HA 1988 s. 9
41 The Rents Act (County Court proceedings for Possession) Rules 1981
42 The County Court Rules 1981, Order 24, and Rules of the Supreme Court, Order 113
43 HA 1988 s. 31
44 HA 1985 s. 80
45 HA 1985 s. 81
46 HA 1985 Sch. 1
47 HA 1985 s. 83
48 Secure Tenancies (Notices) Regulations, 1980, S.I. 1980, No. 1339
49 HA 1985 s. 84 and Sch. 2, Part 1
50 HA 1985 Sch. 2, Part IV
51 HA 1985 Sch. 24
52 LTA 1954 s. 4
53 LTA 1954 ss. 12-14
54 MHA 1983 s. 1
55 MHA 1983 Sch. 1
56 Caravan Sites Act 1968 ss. 3-4
57 MHA Sch. 1
58 MHA s. 1

59 MHA Sch. 1
60 MHA ss. 4 and 5(1)(a)
61 CLA 1977 s. 10
62 CLA 1977 s. 7

Chapter 3

1 RA 1977 s. 70
2 RA 1977 s. 44
3 RA 1977 s. 49
4 RA 1977 ss. 77-85
5 HA 1988 ss. 13-14
6 HA 1988 ss. 22
7 LTA 1985 ss. 18-30A
8 HA 1985 s. 24
9 HBR 1987, Reg. 3
10 HBR 1987, Reg. 10 and Sch. 1
11 HBR 1987, Reg. 10 and Sch. 1
12 HBR 1987, Reg. 10(1)
13 HBR 1987, Sch. 1
14 HBR 1987, Reg. 11(1)
15 HBR 1987, Sch. 1
16 HBR 1987, Reg. 11
17 HBR 1987, Regs. 2 and 13-15
18 HBR 1987, Regs. 76-77
19 HBR 1987, Reg. 90
20 HBR 1987, Reg. 93
21 HBR 1987, Reg. 66
22 HBR 1987, Reg. 5
23 HBR 1987, Regs. 79-87
24 HBR 1987, Regs. 46-60
25 HBR 1987, Reg. 5

Chapter 4

1 PHA 1936 s. 92
2 PHA 1936 s. 93
3 PHA 1936 s. 94
4 Building Act 1984 s. 76
5 PHA 1961 s. 17
6 HA 1985 s. 604(1)
7 HA 1985 ss. 189-208
8 HA 1985 ss. 192 and 264-282
9 HA 1985 s. 606
10 LTA 1985 s.17(1), County Courts Acts 1984 s. 22 and Defective Premises Act 1972 s. 4

11 HA 1985 ss. 209-238
12 HA 1985 ss. 324-344
13 HA 1985 s. 345
14 HA 1985 s. 352
15 HA 1985 s. 776
16 HA 1985 ss. 352-364
17 HA 1985 ss. 365-368
18 S.I. 1981 No. 1576
19 HA 1985 ss. 369-373
20 HA 1985 ss. 379-394 and Sch. 13
21 DoE Circular 21/84
22 HA 1985 s. 96
23 HA 1985 ss. 460-526
24 HA 1985 ss. 521-522

Chapter 5

1 PEA 1977 ss. 1 and 3 and HA 1987 ss. 27-33
2 HA 1980 Sch. 25
3 RA 1977 Sch. 1
4 LTA 1985 ss. 4-5
5 LTA 1985 s. 11(6)
6 RA 1977 s. 116
7 RA 1977 s. 124
8 RA 1977 ss.124
9 LTA 1987, Part 1
10 LTA 1987, Part II
11 LTA 1987, Part IV
12 HA 1985 ss. 87 and 89
13 HA 1985 s. 113
14 HA 1985 ss. 93-94
15 HA 1985 ss. 91 and 95
16 HA 1985 ss. 97-99 and s. 109
17 HA 1985 s. 105
18 HA 1985 ss. 102-103
19 HA 1985 s. 104
20 HA 1985 s. 106
21 HA 1985 ss. 118-188
22 HA 1985 ss. 143-153
23 HA 1988, Part IV

Chapter 6

1 CoG para. 2.10b
2 CoG para. 2.16
3 HA 1985 s. 67

Index

Figures in **bold** type indicate pages on which legal and technical terms are described.

Accommodation agencies, 28, 46-49
Agricultural workers, 64-66, 72
Almshouses, 82
Armed forces, landlord member of, 60
Assigning a tenancy, see: *Council tenants, Housing Association tenants and Private tenants*
Assured tenancies, 67-72
Attendances, 54, 61

Bailiffs, 78
Battered women, see: *Violence, domestic*
Bed and Breakfast hotels, 44, 113, 131-3
Board, **53**, 61, 72
Board and lodging allowance, 113
Building societies, 32
Business lettings **55,** 82
Buying a home, see *Home ownership*

Campaigning, 168-9
Charity landlord, 82, 84, 153
Citizens' Advice Bureaux, 164
Company lettings, 55
Compensation for loss of home, 21
Compulsory purchase orders, 21, 86
Controlled tenancies, 53
Control orders, 132
Conveyancing, 40-41
Co-operatives, 30-31
  security for tenants of management co-ops, 79-85
Council tenants, 14-27, 79-85, 99, 133-137, 149-154
  assigning a tenancy, 151
  allocations, 14-22
  consultation, right to, 152
  distraint, 99
  elderly, special schemes for, 22
  exchanges, 24-26
  eviction, 79-85
  hard to let schemes, 22
  homelessness, see: *Homelessness*
  housing lists, 15-16
  improvements, 151
  information, rights to, 152
  inheriting a tenancy 149-150
  key worker schemes, 22
  licensees, 80, 137
  lodgers, 150
  mobility schemes, 26-27
  National Mobility Scheme, 26
  notice of seeking possession, 82
  offers of housing, 22
  racial harassment, 24
  rent, 24, 99
  rent arrears, 82-83, 99
  repairs, 22, 133-137
  right to buy, 152-154
  right to exchange, 24-25
  right to register, 14
  right to rehousing, 21
  security for tenants, 79-85
  subtenants, 150
  succession, 149-150
  suitable alternative accommodation, 83, 84, 85, 150
  tenancy agreements, 24, 152
  tenants' associations, 171
  tied housing, 81, 83
  transfers, 24, 151
  waiting lists, 15-16
Crown tenants, 55, 80

Defective Premises Act 1972, 126
Deposits, 29
Direction orders, 132
Disability, 17, 27, 29, 44, 84, 139, 153
Distraint, 99
Disrepair, see: *Repairs*
Disturbance payments, 21
Divorce, see: *Relationship break up*

Elderly people, 22, 29
  leasehold for the elderly, 42
  sheltered housing, 22, 42
Endowment mortgages, see: *Home ownership*
Estate agents, see: *Home ownership*
Eviction, see: *Council tenants, Housing association tenants and Private tenants*
Exchanges, 24-27

Fair rents, 91-94, 147
Farm workers, see: *Agricultural workers*
Fire brigade housing, 81
Fire, means of escape from, 132
  special grants, 138
Flat agencies, see: *Accommodation agencies*

General Improvement Areas, 129
Government departments, tenants of, 55

Harassment, 143-145
Homelessness, 16-20, 43-45
 advice and assistance, 18
 criminal offences, 20
 furniture storage, 20
 injunctions against violence, 156-158
 intentional homelessness, 17-18, 156
 local connection, 18-19
 offers of accommodation, 20
 priority need, 17
 resettlement units, 115
 single homeless campaign, 169
 temporary accommodation, 19, 43-45, 81
 threatened with homelessness, 16
 violence, 16, 17, 19, 156-158
 vulnerability, 17
Home loss payment, 21
Home ownership, 31-43, 86-7, 100-103
 banks, 32, 33
 building societies, 32
 buying a home, 31-43
 conveyancing, **40**-41
 deposits, 41
 endowment mortgages, 33, 35, 102
 estate agents, 33, 39, 48, 49
 exchange of contracts, 41
 Home Loan Scheme, 101
 homesteading, 42
 insurance, 37-8, 41
 insurance companies, 33, 35
 Land Registry fees, 37
 leaseholds, 37, **38,** 42, 86-87, 96-98
 mortgages, **32**-36, 38-40, 100-103
 mortgage arrears, 86, 103
 mortgage brokers, 33
 part possession, 38
 rates, 37
 rental purchase, 42
 retentions, 36
 service charges, **37**
 sex discrimination, 34, 49
 shared ownership, 41, 153
 solicitors, 36-37, 40-41
 stamp duty, 37
 surveys, 40
 tax relief, 100-101
 valuations, 36 39
Hostels, 43, 113, 131-133
Hotels, 44, 113, 131-133
Houses in Multiple Occupation, 131-133, 138-142, 169
Housing Action Areas, 129
 grants, 138-142
Housing advice centres, 164-165
Housing association tenants, 29-30, 79-85, 100, 117-133, 149-154
 assigning a tenancy, 151
 consultation, right to, 152
 eviction, 67-72, 79-85
 exchange, rights to, 24-25
 improvements, 151
 information, rights to, 152
 inheriting a tenancy, 149-150
 lodgers, 150
 moving to another area, 30
 notice of seeking possession, 82
 rent, 100
 rent arrears, 82-83, 100
 repairs, 117-129, 133
 right to buy, 152-154
 security for tenants, 67-72, 79-85
 shared ownership, 51, 153
 sheltered housing, 43-44
 subtenants, 150
 succession, 149-150
 suitable alternative accommodation, 70, 83, 84, 85, 150
 tenancy agreements, changes to, 152
 tied housing, 71, 81, 83
 transfers, 30, 151
Housing benefit, 103-116
 appeals, 108-109
 heating charges, 105
 income disregards, 106
 lodgers, 104-105
 non-dependants, 104-105, 110
 payment method, 107
 review boards, 108-109
 service charges, 105-106
 students, 109-110
 subtenants, 104-105
 tapers, 107, 112
 water rates, 105

Immigrants, 116, 165-166
Improvements, 101, 127-129, 131-133, 138-142
 improvement Grants, 138-142
 insulation Grants, 142
Injunctions against violence, 156-158

Joint tenants, **73,** 151

Law Centres, 165
Leasehold, see: *Home ownership*

Legal Aid, see: *Solicitors*
Licensees, see: *Council tenants and Private tenants*
Local authority tenants, see: *Council tenants*
Lodgers, 51, 104-105, 150-151

Management Orders, 132
Marriage break up, see: *Relationship break up*
Mobile homes, 87-89
Mortgages, see *Home ownership*

National Mobility Scheme, 26
New Towns, 27
  security for tenants, 79-85
  shared ownership in, 41
Notice of seeking possession, 82
Notice to Quit, 57, 94

Ombudsman, Local Government, 135
One parent families, 165
Overcrowding, 55, 83, 129-131, 131-132, 147
Owner occupation, see: *Home ownership*

Police housing, 81
Private tenants, 27-29, 50-79, 117-133, 138-142, 142-149
  armed forces, landlord member of, 60
  assigning a tenancy, 58
  assured tenants, 67-72
  attendance, **53-54,** 61
  board, **53,** 61
  business lettings, **55**
  children not allowed, 147
  company lettings, **55**
  contractual tenancies, 56
  controlled tenancies, 53
  deposits, 29
  exclusive possession, **52**
  eviction, 50-79
  eviction, illegal, 144-145
  fair rents, 91-94, 147
  fixed term tenancies, 56
  flat sharers, 73-75
  fuel charges, 148
  furniture, 29, 58, 147
  harassment, 143-145
  holiday lettings, **54,** 59, 72
  improvements, 127-129, 131-133
  inheriting a tenancy, 145
  inventory, 29, 147
  joint tenants, **73,** 151
  landlord's right to enter, 146
  landlord, right to know name of, 149
  lease, see: *Tenancy agreement*
  licensees, **51-52,** 75, 75-76, 145-146
  mortgage, landlord with, 75
  Notice to Quit, 57, 94
  payments in advance, 29
  periodic tenancies, **56**
  possession, see: *Eviction*
  protected tenants, see: *Regulated tenants*
  racial discrimination, 46-48
  reasonable rents, 94-95
  Regulated Tenants, **53**-60, 91-94
  Rent Act 1977, 53-62
  rent arrears, 57
  Rent Assessment Committee, 94, 95-6
  rent books, 145-146
  Rent Officer, 91-94
  Rent Tribunal, 94-95
  resident landlords **54**-55, 68, 72
  restricted protection, **60**-62, 76, 94-95
  retirement home, landlord's, 59
  returning owner occupier, 59
  service charges, 96-98
  service occupiers and service tenants, **63**-66
  sharers, 73-75
  shared living accommodation, 55, 72
  shorthold, **62**-63, **71**
  statutory tenancy, 56
  student lettings, **54,** 59, 68, 70
  subletting, 58, **73**-75
  succession, 145
  suitable alternative accommodation, 58, 70-71
  tenancy agreement, 28-29, 52, 147-148
  tied housing, 63-66
  agricultural workers, 64-66
Protected tenants, see: *Private tenants*
Public Health Acts, see: *Repairs*

Racial discrimination, 46-48, 168
Racial Harassment, 24
Rates, 24, 37
  rates rebates, 103-113
Regulated tenants, see: *Private tenants*
Relationship break up, 155-163, 168
  custody of children, 162-163
  injunctions, 156-158
  maintenance, 162
  rights to the home, 158-161
  violence, 16, 17, 19, 156-158
Reasonable rents for restricted contract tenants, 94-95
Rental purchase, 42, 143

Rents, see *Council tenants, Housing association tenants and Private tenants*
Rent arrears, 57, 82-83, 99, 100, 162
Rent Officer, 91-94
Repairs, 117-127, 133-142
abatement notices, 119
closing order, 121
court action, 123-126
council tenants, 22, 133-137
demolition order, 121
Environmental Health Officer, 123
grants, 138-142
Housing Acts, 120-122
Housing association tenants, 117-129, 133
landlord's responsibilities, 117-118
nine day notice, 119
private tenants, 117-127
Public Health Acts, 118-119, 128
reasonable expense, 120-121
recurring nuisance, 119
statutory nuisance, 118-119
unfit properties, 120-122
withholding rent, 126-127
Resettlement units, 115
Resident landlord, **54**-55, 68, 72
Restricted protection, see: *Private tenants*
Retirement home, landlord's, 59
Right to buy, 152-154

Service charges, 37, 96-98, 105-106
Sex discrimination, 34, 48-49
Shared ownership, see: *Home ownership*
Sheltered housing, 22, 43-44
Shorthold, **62**-63, **71**
Short life housing, 45, 81
Social Security, 101-2. 103-105, 113
Solicitors, 36-37, 40-41, 76-77, 166
Squatting, 44-45, 89-90
Student lettings, **54,** 59, 68, 70
Subtenants, see: *Council tenants, Housing association tenants and Private tenants*

Temporary accommodation, 20, 43-45, 82, 140
bed and breakfast hotels, 44, 113, 131-3
hostels, 43, 113, 131-133
short life housing, 45, 81
squatting, 44-45, 89-90
women's refuge, 44, 165
Tenancy agreements, see: *Council tenants, Housing association tenants and Private tenants*
Tenancy Relations Officer, 144-145
Tenants' co-operatives, see: *Co-operatives*
Tied housing, see: *Council tenants, Housing Association tenants and Private tenants*
Transfers, 24, 151

Violence, domestic, 16, 17, 19, 156-158

Welfare rights, 165, 169 (see also: *Housing Benefit and Social Security)*
Well maintained payment, 21
Women's refuges, 44, 165